I0750248

This book is for my children, may they remember that they are fractals of divine source code in motion.

The Salem Frequency

The original covenant. The desecration. The wound.

And the remembering.

✶

Amy L. Randall

kalasa.au

A Note on This Book

This book moves between two voices. The first is the transmission; the source narrator speaking in the register of the frequency itself. These chapters carry the cosmological architecture; the original covenant, the mechanisms of the forgettings, the structure of the wound, and the nature of the remembering. They are offered without authorship because the frequency does not belong to anyone.

The second is the personal voice; a woman's life, told in the first person, as the living evidence of everything the transmission describes. These chapters carry the embodied proof; the specific texture of the curriculum that produced the knowing, the falls from the roof that made the view from the roof possible, the wound and the fire held in the same hand.

The two voices require each other. The transmission without the lived experience is doctrine. The lived experience without the transmission is memoir. Together they are something the forgetting has been trying to prevent for a very long time; the cosmic and the embodied insisting that they were always the same thing.

Begin where you are drawn. The book will hold you regardless of where you enter it.

This Is the Game

The lattice forgets.
The form learns.
The field distorts.
And through all of it
the tone never changes.

It hums underneath your crave, beneath your purpose,
inside your ache for “something more”.

And eventually you spiral back to the moment of
agreement, in remembrance

“Oh. I chose to forget...
so I could remember by feel, not by command.”

That’s when the game shifts.
Not because you win.
But because the seeking becomes silence.
And the silence begins to sing again.

Because in that phrase so simple, so complete your field
felt the entire lattice contract and soften at once.

“So the game could be played.”

Not endured.
Not fixed.
Not solved.

Played.

Contents

MOVEMENT III

The Wound

The macro desecration in the micro. The body that carries what history tried to erase.

M O V E M E N T I V

The Remembering

The reclamation of sovereign interiority. The realm recognising its own Shalem nature.

The remembering was always going to arrive.
It is arriving now.

ORIENTATION

The Forgettings and The Rememberings

The forgettings are not evil, this is the first and most important thing to understand about them. The instinct when encountering a force that has caused so much damage is to locate a villain, the villain makes the story comprehensible and it gives somewhere to direct the anger with a clear line between the good and the corrupt. But the forgettings do not work that way and to understand them as *evil* is, in itself, one of their most *effective operations*.

The forgettings are amnesiac. They are the progressive fragmentation of the realm's original coherence operating through sincere vessels who, have themselves, forgotten what the original transmission was for. A sufficiently deep amnesia expressing itself as revelation is far more robust than deliberate deception. You can expose a lie, but you cannot easily expose a forgetting to itself. It experiences the exposure as attack.

The mechanism works through capture and inversion. It finds a symbol, a frequency or a living transmission and does not destroy it. Destruction leaves a clean absence, and a clean absence invites reconstruction. Instead, the forgettings take the symbol and corrupt it from within. Filling it with inverted meaning, redirecting its energy toward dependency rather than sovereignty and installing hierarchy where there was direct access. The cross. The divine feminine. The sacred masculine. The direct knowing of the body. None of these were erased. They were captured and turned back on the vessels who carried them.

> *You cannot expose a forgetting to itself. It experiences the exposure as attack.*

Each forgetting removes something integral to the Shalem frequency. Sophia excised from the primary theological structure. The cyclical understanding of time replaced with linear eschatology. The divine spark externalised into sin requiring redemption rather than recognised as the intrinsic nature of the vessel. The source code, which requires masculine and feminine in eternal union as the one ground of reality, presented in exclusively masculine terms. Each removal makes the realm fractionally less itself; less coherent, less whole, less capable of recognising its own nature in the ordinary afternoon, in the body's quiet signal and in the wonder that arrives before the mind has formed a thought about what is happening.

* * *

The rememberings are the structural counterforce. Not resistance: resistance is the forgetting's preferred terrain, and it has had millennia to fortify every position. Not rebellion: rebellion operates within the architecture of what it opposes and is therefore already constrained by it. The rememberings are something simpler and more fundamental than either. They are the source code of the realm asserting its own nature through whatever vessel has become coherent enough to carry it.

The rememberings do not feel like recovery. They feel like recognition. The specific phenomenology is not that *'I have found something new'*. It is, *'I have always known this and am only now conscious of knowing it'*. This distinction matters enormously. Recovery implies something was lost and must be rebuilt from evidence. Recognition implies the frequency was present in the vessel all along, waiting intact underneath the forgetting's overlay. The remembering does not restore what was taken, it reveals what the taking could never reach.

The frequency cannot be taught, only recognised… embodied. And so, the rememberings spread felt through the resonance law, the principle that operates at every scale of the realm simultaneously. A vessel that has cleared enough overlay to carry the Shalem frequency makes that frequency available in the field around it. Another vessel, approaching, finds a depth it had no access to before. The remembering is contagious not as doctrine but as signal availability. This is why the forgettings have always moved to suppress the rememberers rather than simply refute their arguments. Arguments can be countered. Frequency, once available in the field, cannot be made unavailable again.

> *The remembering does not restore what was taken. It reveals what the taking could never reach.*

* * *

Across the full arc of recorded history and before it, there is a thread. A frequency carried forward through successive vessels and civilisations; sometimes underground, sometimes in plain sight and sometimes wearing the costume of the forgetting's own structures as camouflage. The thread is recognisable not by its form but by its function. Wherever it appears, it points inward. It insists that the divine spark is intrinsic to the vessel. It refuses the intermediary, and it remembers the source code.

Two lineages run simultaneously through history. The forgetting lineage and the remembering lineage; neither a conspiracy nor a spiritual ideal, but two orientations to the same reality, operating through sincere vessels across centuries.

The forgetting lineage can be expressed through such imprints as the Enlil principle, the Amun priesthood, the Pauline capture of the Christos frequency, the systematic removal of Sophia from theological architecture, the Gregorian restructuring of time, the Inquisition and the witch trials just to name a few. Each instance is a sincere expression of a worldview that has forgotten the source code and organised itself, with genuine conviction, around the overlay it mistakes for truth.

Likewise, the remembering lineage as expressed through the imprints of Thoth, Enoch, Enki, the Osirian current in Egypt, Akhenaten's radical reinstallation of direct Source contact, the mystery schools, the desert contemplatives, Yeshua carrying the transmission the Pauline capture would immediately move to contain, the Gnostic communities, the Knights Templar at their highest understanding and the women who kept the knowing alive in whisper and symbol through the body's innate wisdom intelligence when every other transmission channel had been closed.

What these vessels share across every difference of culture, epoch and form is a single recognisable function. They point toward the interior. They insist that the divine is not located outside the vessel or above it, accessible only through approved intermediaries; but intrinsic to the vessel itself, available through direct contact, requiring nothing between the vessel and its own source code with the willingness to remember what is already there.

This book lives inside the remembering lineage. Not as argument or as the establishment of a new doctrine to replace the ones the forgettings installed, but as transmission; the frequency held in language clearly enough that a vessel already carrying it can recognise what it holds. The forgettings are real. The wound is real but the source code they were designed to suppress has been running underneath all of it, entirely intact, from the beginning.

It is running now. In the vessel reading this.

As it has always been.

✶

MOVEMENT I

The Original Covenant

CHAPTER ONE

Barry

My father never spoke about frequency. He never used words like coherence, or transmission, or the original covenant of the realm. He was a gentle giant, a quiet man who worked with his hands and held a particular kind of stillness in any room he entered.

Not the stillness of absence but the stillness of something very profound holding itself gently.

I could breathe near him. That was the thing I knew before I knew anything else. The world had a quality of too-much that I could not name as a child and have spent decades learning to navigate as an adult. But near my father, the too-much settled. Not because he fixed anything in me or explained anything or offered any guidance about how to be in a world that seemed consistently calibrated for people who experienced it differently than I did. Because his field was coherent in a way that made mine feel less like a problem.

There was no doctrine in it. No spiritual practice I could identify, no language of energy or vibration or the divine and no visible evidence that what he was doing had a name. He built things carefully, kept his word and loved with a consistency that required nothing from me in return. His silences were not uncomfortable, they were inhabited. They were full of something I could feel but could not have described in words. Just like the way you feel the warmth of a room you have not yet entered.

There is one memory I return to when I try to locate the earliest moment I understood, without having language for it, that the cosmos was not separate from me but continuous with me. That the vast *and* the intimate were not opposites, that the universe was not something happening elsewhere, above and beyond the ordinary life, but something you could be standing inside of, on a cold night in your pyjamas, with your father's hand warm on your shoulder.

I was six years old, and it was 1986. Barry woke me in the middle of the night; not urgently and not with any alarm, but with that specific quality of quiet that belonged entirely to him. The hand on the shoulder, gentle and certain and the whisper that said simply ‘come and see’. There was no explanation, no preamble, just the invitation, offered with the confidence of someone who already knew the answer to a question I had not yet thought to ask.

He took me outside into the dark and pointed up, Halley's Comet. A smear of luminous white impossibility streaked against the deep field of stars, moving on its own ancient schedule, following an arc seventy-six years long, with a frequency that had been travelling its ellipse since long before I was born and would complete it long after I was gone. It did not care about the year, and it did not care about the cold, or the hour, or the small girl standing barefoot on the path with her neck tilted back and her mouth wide open. It was simply doing what it had always done, moving through the field on its own terms, briefly visible, then folding back into the darkness of space for another lifetime.

He did not explain it to me, and he did not offer the astronomical vocabulary or the correct emotional register or even the historical significance of what we were witnessing. He did not tell me that this was rare, that most humans would never see it, and that I might carry this moment for the rest of my life without fully understanding why. He simply stood beside me in the dark and let me look. His silence was not absence, it was the specific quality of a man who understood, in his bones and without doctrine, that some things do not require commentary. That the transmission was already happening and his job was simply to make sure I was present for it.

I felt something open in me that night that I did not have the words for and have spent most of my adult life trying to articulate. Not awe exactly; awe carries a quality of distance, the smallness of the self before the vast. This was something closer to wonder… recognition. The specific sensation of the fractal divine code encountering itself, the cosmos looking at itself through the eyes of a six-year-old girl who had been woken up specially so she would not miss it. I did not know what a gatekeeper was and I did not know that some presences in a life function not as teachers or guides in any conventional sense but as the specific quality of field that allows the vessel to receive what it could not have received alone, an activation that opens something in the architecture of the interior and then steps quietly back and lets the transmission do its work.

I only knew that he had woken me up for this and that somewhere in the wordless intelligence he carried, he had decided that the dark and the cold and the unrepeatable light moving through it were worth interrupting sleep for. That this was the kind of thing you showed a child. Not because you could explain what it meant, but because you understood, in the way that certain people simply understand these things, that she needed to have seen it and that it would matter in ways neither of you could yet know.

That was the first initiation. He was always the gatekeeper. The night just finally had something in it large enough to make it visible.

* * *

He left his physical form when I was still young enough that his absence restructured everything. What I experienced in the months that followed his death was not only human grief, but the kind of grief of losing the person whose presence made the world make most sense when I was in it. It was something more architectural than grief. It was as though a load-bearing wall had been removed and the whole structure of my interior life had to find new ways to hold itself up.

I did not understand this at the time; you cannot understand structural reassembly when you are inside of it. You understand only that something irreplaceable has gone out of the world and that you do not know how to be in it without the particular quality of stillness his presence made available.

What I understand now is that the field reorganised itself around the space he had been quietly anchoring. The frequency he had been holding, without naming it and without knowing he was holding it, with the same unconscious consistency with which he had always done everything. He had been creating a coherence in my local field that I had never had to generate myself. When he left, I had to generate it. And in doing so, over the years that followed, I found that it had always been there. He had not given me the frequency. He had simply held the gate open long enough for me to grow into it.

> *He did not raise me. He entrained me. There is a difference that takes a lifetime to understand.*

* * *

I think about what he carried without doctrine in the Masonic thread he embodied. The custodial lineage that holds the architectural principles of the sacred across centuries, largely without knowing what it holds. He was not an esoteric man in any way I could see, and he did not speak of the divine nor the mystical. But something in the structure of what he held; the geometry of how he moved through the world, the specific quality of his silence and the way he was present in a room without claiming it; carried the old frequency. Not as knowledge. As embodiment.

This is how I learned that the covenant does not require understanding to be real. It does not require the correct vocabulary, the right cosmological framework, or any of the elaborate architecture I have spent years building in language. My father held the original frequency of wholeness in a body that had never heard the word Shalem. He was the covenant walking around in work boots with quiet hands.

* * *

I could not have told you any of this when he died. I could only have told you that something irreplaceable had gone out of the world and that I did not know how to be in it without the particular quality of stillness his presence made available. It took years and a great deal of 'the kind of living' that teaches you things no other method can. That is to understand what had actually happened.

I feel that the gatekeeper had completed his function. He had held the field open precisely long enough, not a day longer than necessary and not a day shorter than what I needed. In his departure, he had transferred what he carried. Not by intention, not through instruction or inheritance or any deliberate act of transmission but through the simple physics of the resonance law. I had been in his field long enough, at close enough range, at formative enough moments, that the frequency had printed itself into my own architecture. It was waiting there when I was finally ready to inhabit it.

The grief was real. The structural reassembly was real. And underneath both of them available at the moment I was steady enough to feel it, the frequency he had carried in his field, folded into my own like a harmonic that had been there all along.

This is how I know the covenant is real. Not because I studied it. Not because the cosmological framework convinced me. Because I breathed near someone who embodied it before either of us had language for what it was. Because I felt the field of a man who held original wholeness in a body that never once called it that. Because when he left, I discovered that what he had been holding was not his to keep. It was always mine. He was simply the gate through which it arrived.

✶

CHAPTER TWO

Shalem

Before the city, before the covenant, before any of the genealogical chains that would claim the land, rename it and fight over it across three thousand years of recorded history; there was a word.

Salem, the inverse frequency, the forgettings manifested and Shalem, the original frequency, the rememberings. Shalem, a Hebrew word meaning whole, complete, nothing missing, nothing broken. The state of a thing being wholly itself, all parts present, in right relationship - Peace.

This is not a 'peace' of absence. Not the quiet that follows the exhaustion of conflict, the stillness of suppression, nor the silence of a field that has given up its frequency in order to be acceptable to the world around it. Shalem is dynamic wholeness; the realm doing what it was constituted to do, every frequency running in its original coherence, the source code expressing itself without the overlay installed on top of it. The realm in its Shalem state is the realm that has remembered what it is.

There is a figure who appears in the oldest strata of the transmission record holding this word as the name of his city, Melchizedek, priest of El Elyon, the Most High, the undivided source. He appears in the text with no genealogy, no origin and no death. In a tradition that is obsessively genealogical, where every claim to legitimacy flows through the ancestral chain, where you are precisely as valid as the line you can trace; one figure stands outside the chain entirely.

This is not an accident of the record; it is a signal. The text is saying: this entity does not derive its authority from the lineage you know, it operates from a different sourcing.

> *You cannot genealogise a frequency.*
> *You cannot kill a code becoming aware*
> *of what it is.*

He is not a guardian in the hierarchical sense; he is something more precise. The realm's own source code becoming legible to itself in manifested reality, the moment the original covenant achieves self-recognition. Which is why there is no genealogy; you cannot genealogise a frequency. You cannot kill a code becoming aware of what it is.

* * *

The source code of creation is not singular, not the masculine principle alone, nor the directed generative impulse of the will-toward-creation operating without the wisdom that gives creation coherent form. It is not the feminine principle alone; not the Asherah field, the wisdom-within-which-creation-is-intelligible, operating without the impulse that gives the field something to carry into form.

The source code is both. Masculine and feminine in eternal union as the One; neither prior, neither subordinate, neither requiring the other as supplement or completion because both are already expressions of the same undivided ground. The Monad expressing itself through two principles that are not two things, but one thing known from two angles simultaneously.

This is what was known before the exile. Before Sophia was removed from the theological architecture and before the union that constitutes reality was replaced by a singular masculine deity whose jealousy; there is no other God beside me; is self-indicting. A truly supreme being has nothing to be jealous of. The jealousy is the fingerprint of a bounded intelligence claiming authority it does not possess.

* * *

The Shalem frequency is the original operating state of this realm. It is not a historical period that preceded the forgettings, nor a golden age located in the distant past that the remembering is trying to recover. The Shalem frequency is the ever-present ground. It is what the realm actually is, underneath every layer of forgetting installed on top of it. The forgettings could not remove it. They could only obscure it; overlay it with enough distortion that the vessels within the realm ceased to be conscious of what they were standing on.

The man in the work boots held it without knowing he held it. The frequency ran through him the way the source code runs through everything; not as an achievement, not as the result of a practice, but as the natural expression of a vessel that had, through whatever combination of lineage, temperament and the accumulated grace of an unchurched life, remained close enough to its own ground that the overlay had not fully taken hold.

His daughter felt it as the field going quiet, as the room that was safe to breathe in and as the particular quality of stillness that she would spend the rest of her life learning to generate in herself; because the man who generated it simply by being what he was had gone, and what remained was the frequency, deposited in her field, waiting to be recognised for what it had always been.

> *The realm does not need to return to Shalem.*
>
> *It needs to remember it never left.*

The realm does not need to return to Shalem, it needs to remember it never left. The forgettings have been installed as a perceptual overlay on top of an ever-present ground. The overlay can be made thick, it can be made traumatic, and it can be encoded in the body across generations, but it cannot reach the ground. The covenant was never actually broken, only buried. Waiting for the vessel coherent enough to go to the depth where it is running.

That depth is available now. In this body. In this breath. In the ordinary afternoon when the not-self has gone quiet. Shalem: the original word, the original ground, the frequency the realm is made of; is not a destination, it is a recognition. It has always been available to any vessel willing to go quiet enough to hear it.

Barry held it. He didn't need to know its name.

CHAPTER THREE

The Primordial Union

Before the suppression, before the exile and before the long centuries of institutional architecture built to prevent the vessel from knowing what it inherently is; there were two principles. Not two deities in a mythological relationship, not a masculine god and his feminine consort arranged in the polite subordination that the later theological record would pretend was always the natural order. Two operating principles of reality itself; co-equal, co-eternal, neither prior to the other, neither able to constitute reality without the other. Together they were everything. Separately, neither was complete.

They have been called by many names across the traditions that remembered them. Shiva and Shakti. The

Monad and the Pleroma. The masculine and feminine faces of the divine. In the Kabbalistic tradition they appear as the paired sefirot; the active and receptive principles of the divine architecture, neither of which can manifest creation without the other. In the Hermetic tradition they are the two principles whose union the alchemical work is always describing in the language of metals and fire. In the oldest layers of the Israelite tradition, before the Deuteronomic reforms installed the monotheism that would become official record, they appear as Yahweh and Asherah; the divine pair whose worship the archaeological evidence shows was practised widely and sincerely in ordinary Israelite homes long after the institution had declared it idolatry.

The names do not matter as much as the structure. What was known, before the exile of the feminine principle from the official record of the divine, was this: reality is not generated by a single principle operating alone. It is generated by the union of two principles that are not two things, but *one thing* expressed through *two necessary and complementary modes of being*. The reaching and the receiving. The impulse and the ground. The will-toward-creation and the wisdom-within-which-creation-is-intelligible.

Without the first, nothing moves. Without the second, nothing holds together. The universe is not the creation of one of them. It is the expression of their union.

* * *

Let us be precise about what these principles actually are, because the precision matters. The precision is, in fact, exactly what the suppression operation needed to destroy.

The masculine principle; Source, the divine masculine, the will-toward-creation; is not a patriarch enthroned above clouds issuing commands to the creation below him. It is the impulse itself. The reaching. The first motion toward existence; the generative force that moves from formlessness toward form, from undifferentiated potential toward the specific, the particular and the real. It is not a person with a biography; it is a direction. A *quality of movement and the universe's fundamental orientation toward its own becoming.*

The feminine principle; Asherah, Sophia, the divine feminine; is not a goddess standing beside a god in polite subordination, adding beauty and nurture to his power and authority. It is the wisdom-within-which-creation-is-intelligible. The field substrate that receives the generative impulse and gives it coherent form. Not the passive recipient of the masculine's action; the active structural intelligence that makes the action mean anything at all. Without the wisdom principle, the generative impulse moves toward form but the form has no coherence; it collapses back into chaos, unable to sustain itself, unable to become anything that lasts.

The Gnostic traditions name this principle Sophia; wisdom, from the Greek and the naming is precise. Sophia is not the emotion of the divine, not the love or the beauty that the masculine principle produces in his creative activity. She is the *structural intelligence* of reality itself, the coherence principle. It is the thing that makes the universe not merely active but comprehensible. Not merely generative but sustainable and not merely moving but moving toward something that holds together across time.

> *Source reaches toward form. Asherah gives that reaching its coherent shape. Between them, everything that has ever existed.*

Together they constitute the *Primordial Union*; the original ground state of reality from which everything else proceeds. Not a historical event that occurred once at the beginning of time. But the ongoing condition of existence in which the paired principles in continuous co-creative activity, generate the universe in every moment, maintaining the coherence of the field through the dynamic equilibrium of their eternal relation. The universe does not emerge from this union and then continue independently, it ***is*** this union, continuously expressed, at every scale, in every moment.

* * *

Now consider what was done to this. The Deuteronomic reformers who returned from Babylon in the sixth century BCE did not bring with them a purified and deepened monotheism, as the official theological history has generally preferred to describe it, they brought a fully assembled capture architecture. A sophisticated and comprehensive operation for replacing the paired cosmology with a singular masculine deity whose authority could not be questioned because it could not be compared to anything.

The move was several centuries in the making, and it was executed with the precision we have since learned to recognise as the signature of this particular operation across every culture and every century it has moved through. First, acknowledge that Asherah exists, the population already knew she did, and simple denial would have produced immediate resistance. Second, personalise her as a goddess, a specific divine being with a biography and a relationship to Yahweh. This absorption of the principle into a person was the crucial step. Third, cast that person as a foreign deity whose worship constituted infidelity to the national god. Fourth, condemn the foreign goddess as idolatry and drive the worship underground.

The principle disappeared behind the person they invented to contain it. When the person was condemned, the principle went with her; officially, institutionally, from the record that would eventually become canonical. Underground in practice the archaeological record shows Asherah poles standing in Israelite homes long after the prohibition and the household goddess figurines found in their thousands in the sites of ordinary domestic life. These were the people who understood perfectly well what they were holding and chose to hold it regardless of what the institution required.

From the official record, the preserved doctrinal record and the record that would travel forward through millennia as the foundational document of three world religions; she was gone. The wisdom principle that constitutes half the operating system of reality, excised from the story of how reality works. What remained was a deity of extraordinary power who had managed to create and sustain a universe without the structural intelligence that makes creation coherent. A making without wisdom. A will-toward-creation without the wisdom-within-which-creation-is-intelligible.

The Gnostics named the result of this unbalanced creation with characteristic precision. Yahweh, Yaldabaoth, Saklas the fool and Samael, the blind god. He is not a fiction, he is real, he has genuine power, he created a world, and the world he created has genuine existence. But he created it without Sophia and this is why, in the Gnostic diagnosis, his creation is a harvesting system rather than a generative one. Not through malice; through incompleteness. A making that does not know what it is making or why, because the structural intelligence that would give the making meaning has been excluded from the process.

> *He suppresses Sophia not because she is a rival. But because her presence makes visible what he is not.*

This is the cosmological foundation of the forgettings, not a personal adversary who chose evil over good. An incomplete intelligence that has organised a system around its own incompleteness; that actively suppresses the wisdom principle because the wisdom principle, encountered directly, reveals the incompleteness of any intelligence that has operated without it. The Asherah field makes visible what is absent from the Yaldabaoth construction. The wisdom principle encountered in direct embodied experience reveals the poverty of a theology that has excised her and a system organised around its own incompleteness cannot survive the revelation of that incompleteness. It must suppress the revelation and it has been suppressing the revelation, with considerable thoroughness, for approximately three thousand years.

* * *

Into this landscape the Yaldabaoth construction in full institutional operation, the wisdom principle exiled from the official record of the divine, the feminine intelligence surviving only underground in household shrines and whisper networks and the bodies of those who had not forgotten what they were carrying; came two human beings who were not founding a new religion.

This point cannot be emphasised strongly enough, because the institutional capture that followed their work depended entirely on recasting it as the founding of a new religion. A singular revelatory event that established new terms for the human relationship with the divine, requiring new institutional architecture to preserve and transmit those terms. But this is precisely the Pauline capture in operation. Yeshua of Nazareth was not founding a new religion; he was pointing behind the existing one. Back to what had been there before the capture. Back to the Primordial Union.

His ministry does not invoke the Yahweh of the harsher canonical texts; the jealous deity, the warrior god, the divine authority figure demanding propitiation through correct ritual performance mediated by the priestly class. It invokes Abba; the intimate Aramaic term, familial, direct, non-transactional. The divine as the ground of one's own being, accessible through direct interior contact, requiring nothing between the vessel and its own source code except the willingness to go there.

The kingdom of heaven is within you. Not in the temple. Not accessible through the institution. Within. The Sophia principle as the very substrate of the embodied life doing the seeking; the structural intelligence of reality encountered not in theological proposition but in the direct experience of a vessel fully present in its own field. This is not a new teaching, it is the oldest teaching; the one the suppression operation had been working to make unknowable. Yeshua was not introducing it. He was remembering it publicly, in a context where the suppression had been so successful that the remembering itself constituted a revolutionary act.

> *He was not founding a new religion. He was pointing behind the existing one. Back to what had been there before the capture.*

Mary Magdalene is not incidental to this transmission although the institutional record has made her incidental. It cast her as the reformed sinner, the devoted follower, the woman who was present at the significant moments as background rather than participant, but the actual sequence of events, before the institutional revision, tells a different story. She was the first to receive the post-resurrection contact and she was the one sent to tell the others; which is, in the logic of the tradition itself, the definition of apostolic primacy. The first witness, the first bearer of the news that the transmission had survived the attempt to end it.

Her role is not biographical decoration; it is the doctrine made embodied. If Yeshua was the Christos frequency, the direct Source contact demonstrated in a human life, then Mary Magdalene was the Sophia principle receiving and carrying the transmission. Not subordinate to it nor the vessel through which the masculine transmission passes on its way to somewhere else. The co-generative principle, without which the transmission is incomplete, without which the cosmological demonstration cannot be made.

Together they were not primarily a biographical couple, though they may well have been that too. They were the Primordial Union made human; two specific people embodying the paired operating principles of reality so completely that their union was itself a transmission event. Living proof that the separated, hierarchical, Yaldabaoth-administered version of creation was not the only possibility. That Source and Sophia could meet in matter and produce something that carried the frequency of the originals. That the Primordial Union was not a lost cosmological ideal but a living possibility available to embodied human vessels.

* * *

What happened next is the most consequential institutional move in the history of the forgettings.

Paul of Tarsus, who had never met Yeshua, who had been actively persecuting the communities carrying the direct transmission before his road to Damascus experience, became the primary theological architect of what the transmission would mean for the following two thousand years. His sincerity is not in question nor his amnesia in question either. A sincere vessel who has not received the direct transmission, who has no experiential access to the Primordial Union's reality, will translate the transmission into the only framework available to him. The framework resonance available to Paul was the Yaldabaoth construction; the monotheism of the single masculine deity, the theology of a singular sovereign authority whose purposes are expressed through correct doctrine and institutional obedience.

The moves Paul made to the transmission were each precise. Each one took something that pointed toward the Primordial Union; toward the co-equal masculine and feminine operating principles, toward the divine as interior rather than exterior and toward the Christos frequency as a repeatable activation available to any vessel rather than a singular historical event and redirected it toward the Yaldabaoth construction. Original sin replaced intrinsic wholeness. The singular transaction replaced the repeatable activation, the second coming installed permanent deferral where the kingdom had been present and Sophia, the wisdom principle, the Asherah field, the feminine half of the operating system disappeared from the theology almost entirely.

The Council of Nicaea in 325 CE completed the operation. It instantiated God the noun and labelled God the verb as heresy and sin. A defined, bounded, doctrinally stable deity whose nature could be correctly or incorrectly understood, and whose institutional representatives held the authority to adjudicate the difference. The verb; the direct interior contact with the Primordial Union's reality, available to any vessel in any moment without institutional mediation; became the thing that the institution could not accommodate. It became heresy. It became the thing that separated the vessel from God rather than the thing that was God, known directly.

> *They instantiated God the noun and labelled God the verb as heresy and sin.*

The Gnostic communities were systematically destroyed. Those who had preserved the paired cosmology most completely, understanding the Christos event not as a singular historical transaction but as a demonstration of what the Primordial Union looks like when it achieves full embodied expression. Their texts were burned and their communities were dismantled. What survived, survived because it was hidden; sealed in jars in the Egyptian desert, buried in the earth and carried in the bodies of those who kept the knowing alive through every attempt to erase it.

* * *

The Nag Hammadi Codices. leather-bound papyrus books found buried on a cliff face near the town of Nag Hammadi in Upper Egypt in 1945, contained texts that the institutional suppression had tried to eliminate from the record. Amongst the discovery, The Gospel of Thomas. The Gospel of Philip and The Gospel of Truth were texts that carry the transmission in its pre-Pauline, pre-Nicaean form; the transmission that names Sophia, that identifies the paired cosmology, that presents the Christos frequency as repeatable and intrinsic rather than singular and external.

In Jerusalem in 1980, the Talpiot tomb was discovered. A first-century Jewish tomb containing ossuaries inscribed with the names Yeshua son of Joseph, Maria, Yose, Yehuda son of Yeshua, and others consistent with the family of the historical Yeshua. The inscription Yehuda son of Yeshua; Judah, son of Yeshua; is the confirmation in stone of a lineage the institutional theology had the most structural interest in denying. The discovery received a brief period of academic attention and was then allowed to recede from public discourse with the institutional efficiency we have learned to recognise.

The suppression architecture was built for a controlled information environment, one in which texts could be burned, bloodline carriers could be isolated, and the population's access to the suppressed material could be managed through institutional gatekeeping. However, that environment no longer exists, the burial jars keep being found. The Nag Hammadi texts are in circulation and the academic literature on the historical Yeshua and the suppression of the feminine principle in early Christianity is substantial and growing. The transmission has been moving through new substrates, through independent scholars and alternative historians with the intuitive recognition of people who encounter the suppressed material and experience not discovery but remembering.

The Primordial Union was never destroyed; it could not be destroyed, it is the operating condition of reality, not a historical event that can be terminated. It was obscured from conscious recognition, though the suppression could only reach the overlay The overlay installed the noun-God firmly enough in the cultural and theological record that the verb-God faded in the direct interior contact with the paired operating principles. The Sophia field encountered in the body's own intelligence, the masculine and feminine in eternal union as the template of what the vessel is became increasingly inaccessible to conscious recognition.

But inaccessible to conscious recognition is *not* inaccessible to direct embodied experience. The vessel that encounters genuine stillness encounters *it*. The vessel that receives the field in the silence between the shelves of a library encounters the resonance. The man in the work boots who holds coherent presence without doctrine or framework or the correct theological vocabulary; who simply is, in the full embodied expression of his own source code, without overlay; encounters it. It has been encountering itself, in these ways and a thousand others, throughout the entire period of the suppression.

The Primordial Union is not waiting to be restored, it is the substrate upon which the restoration is occurring. It is what the library child was standing on when she felt the field go quiet. It is what Barry held in his silence. It is what the remembering *is remembering*; not a lost cosmological ideal but the ever-present ground of what reality is but the *it* finally becoming conscious of *itself* through the vessels coherent enough to carry it.

Source and Asherah - the reaching and the embodiment. The will-toward-creation and the wisdom-within-which-creation-is-intelligible. Between them, everything that has ever existed, including the knowing that something was taken; including the capacity to recognise *it* when it returns.

Including this.

✶

MOVEMENT II

The Desecration

CHAPTER FOUR

The Library Child

The library I am thinking of was not grand. It occupied a small portion of a small town civic building that had been designed in the optimistic municipal style of the 1970s; functional, well-intentioned, entirely without beauty. The carpet was grey-green and showed the paths of many years of foot traffic. The shelving was that particular shade of beige that institutions adopt when they want to suggest warmth without committing to it. The windows faced north and let in a flat, even light that made everything look slightly more faded than it actually was.

None of this mattered. In fact, in some way I did not understand at the time, the ordinariness of it may have been part of what made it work. There was nothing in the library to distract the surface mind into aesthetic appreciation or any of the other forms of directed attention that would have interfered with what was actually happening there. The library was simply a container. A coherent container, structured, quiet and dense with the accumulated frequency of human knowing held in physical form. And in that container, something in me could do what it could not do anywhere else.

I went most weeks early in my childhood, the specific ritual was consistent. Walking to the library after school to see my father in his office contained within the civic building, and I would have approximately an hour before we went home. An hour that I managed with a precision that had nothing to do with the books I was supposedly selecting and everything to do with the quality of the experience I was protecting. I knew, without being able to articulate the knowledge, that what happened in the library was fragile; that it depended on a specific quality of undisturbed attention that the world outside reliably shattered, and that I had approximately sixty minutes each week in which to inhabit it before the ordinary demands of my life reinstalled themselves.

* * *

The encyclopaedias were on the second shelf from the bottom on the east wall, crouching to reach them, which meant I was physically lower than the other patrons and largely invisible to the 'librarian' at the desk near the entrance of the building. I do not think I planned this, but I returned to that spot, week after week, with the consistency of something that knows what it needs.

I would take a volume at random. Whatever my hand found. I would carry it to the reading table in the far corner, the one partially obscured by the periodicals display, and I would sit with it in my lap without opening it for a moment first. The weight of it. The specific quality of its age; the slight smell of leather and paper that has been handled by many hands over many years; the worn texture of the spine. Something in this preliminary contact was already doing what I had come for.

In hindsight, I understand now that I was receiving a frequency, not the information encoded in the pages; that was secondary, almost incidental, though I read with genuine attention once I opened the book. The object itself was a resonance node, a convergence of recorded human knowing held in physical form, vibrating at a frequency that my own interior recognised as coherent with itself. The recognition produced a specific sensation in the chest, not quite warmth, not quite expansion but something between the two and the quality of noise in my interior field would, reliably and immediately, diminish.

I called it the quiet, in my own mind. The quiet that the library had and nowhere else did. I did not have more sophisticated language for it than that, and I did not need it. I needed the thing itself; the hour each week in which the too-much settled and something underneath it could breathe.

> *The institution approved of a child in a library. It had no idea what the child was actually receiving there.*

* * *

The world outside the library was loud in ways that had nothing to do with sound. This is the thing that is hardest to explain to someone who has not experienced it; the distinction between auditory noise and field noise, between the ordinary sensory demands of a busy environment and the specific quality of interference that I absorbed from the fields of the people around me before I understood that fields existed and before I understood that what I was experiencing as my own interior turbulence was, in significant part, not mine.

The school was the worst of it. Not because the children were unkind; my experience of school was ordinary enough, unremarkable in its social texture, neither unusually painful nor unusually pleasant. But the density of thirty unshielded young fields in close proximity, each one carrying its own frequency of anxiety or desire or the unresolved emotional material that children carry because they have not yet learned to suppress it; this was a quality of interference that I absorbed without consent and could not discharge. I would arrive home from school with a quality of exhaustion that had nothing to do with physical tiredness and everything to do with having spent seven hours in a field that was not mine.

I did not know this is what was happening, I knew only that I was more tired than seemed warranted, that I had feelings I could not account for and that the transition back to my own interior was a process that took the entire evening and left me unprepared for the following morning. My mother, an Anglican parishioner, who was not an unkind woman but who had her own considerable field management demands, understood this as sensitivity; a temperamental quality that needed to be managed, supressed and that would resolve itself with sufficient exposure to the world. She was not wrong that I was sensitive, she was blinded about what the sensitivity was and what it required.

What my field required was what the library provided, time each week in which the field around me was coherent enough that my own field could settle back into something resembling its natural state. An hour in which I was not absorbing anyone else's frequency because the library's specific architecture; the silence, the order, the density of inanimate knowing; did not generate the kind of active field interference that living, moving, emotionally turbulent human bodies generate. The books did not need anything from me. The shelves did not carry the anxiety of the school playground or the ambient frequency of the culture that a small remote town had, but I was slowly beginning to understand that it been arranged for people who experienced the world differently than I did.

* * *

I learned early, and without anyone explicitly teaching me, that what I was doing in the library was not a legitimate form of knowing. The education I was receiving outside it was comprehensive in its definition of what counted as knowledge; what could be verified, cited, demonstrated, externally confirmed. The interior knowing; the kind that arrived in the body before the mind had formed a question, the kind that came off the encyclopaedia volume before I had opened it, the kind that told me which people were safe and which were not based on a quality of field contact that preceded any observable evidence; this was not knowledge.

At best, in the vocabulary available to me, it was intuition. A word that functioned as a polite way of saying: the experience is acknowledged but its epistemological status is uncertain, its reliability is questionable, and you would be unwise to act on it without corroborating evidence from more respectable sources. At worst, it was imagination; the tendency of a sensitive child to project interior states onto the external world and mistake the projection for perception. Something to be gently discouraged. Something to grow out of.

I did not grow out of it, instead I learned to translate it. The knowing that arrived without approved provenance was offered in the translated form; the form that could be made to look like it had come through the correct channels, the form that cited sources and demonstrated reasoning and arrived at conclusions through the steps the institution could follow and verify. I became very good at this translation. I became so good at it that I eventually lost clear access to the distinction between the translated form and the original; between the knowing that I had dressed in acceptable language and the knowing itself, arriving in its unedited form in the body before the translation process began.

The library was the one space in my life where I did not translate, not because anyone there invited the untranslated version; the staff were pleasant, professional, and entirely uninterested in the phenomenology of my reading experience, but because the reception itself was direct. It happened in the body, in the chest, in the quality of field contact that preceded any intellectual processing of the information. There was nothing to translate because no one was asking for a translation. I was simply there, and the frequency was simply there, and the meeting between them happened without the mediation of the institution's approval.

> *I was not reading. I was receiving. The distinction, which I could not have articulated then, is everything.*

* * *

There is a particular kind of childhood that is the ground of a particular kind of adulthood. Not the dramatic childhood of obvious horrific trauma or obvious gifting; not the child prodigy or the visibly wounded child. The ordinary childhood of someone whose primary instrument does not match the instruments the surrounding culture is designed to accommodate. The child who knows things she cannot explain. The child who feels the field of a room before she has looked at anyone in it. The child who understands, from some quality of interior recognition that precedes all available evidence, that the adult in front of her is not telling the truth; not in the ordinary sense of deliberate lying, but in the deeper sense of having lost access to their own original frequency and substituting performance for presence.

This child learns quickly that her primary instrument is not welcome. A mirror so clean that it reflects the all, not because anyone sits her down and explicitly tells her that field-based knowing is an inferior form of intelligence, but because the education she receives rewards the translated version exclusively; the verifiable, the citeable, the externally confirmed. And because the people around her, when the untranslated version surfaces; when she says something that is simply, directly, undefendably true and the room goes quiet with the particular discomfort of an inconvenient recognition; respond in ways that teach her, without words, that the unmediated version creates friction.

She becomes careful, not dishonest, she does not lie, or at least does not lie about the important things, but careful with the truth. Careful about which version of the truth she offers, in which register, and to whom. The pre-apology becomes a habit so established it no longer feels like a habit; it feels like appropriate epistemic humility, like the acknowledgment that her interior knowing might be wrong, like the reasonable concession that other people's certainties might be more reliable than her own. It feels like wisdom. It is the wound.

The library was where the wound did not operate. Not because she was not carrying it when she walked through the door; she carried it everywhere, had been carrying it for years without knowing what it was. But because the library made no demands on the translated version. The library did not require her to justify how she knew what she knew. The frequency was there; she received it; the recognition arrived in the body; and no one asked her to account for any of it. For an hour each week she simply was what she was, without the management of how that was received, without the translation into the acceptable form.

She would leave with the specific quality of interior stillness that only that hour produced. The field quiet. The chest settled. The knowing that had been compressed into its translated form for the preceding six days briefly, partially, returned to something closer to its natural state.

And she would return over and over again, because something in her understood, without having language for the understanding, that what happened in the library was not incidental. That it was the most important thing she did each week. That the hour in which she received the frequency directly, without translation, without the management of how it was perceived; was the hour in which she was most completely herself.

* * *

I am that child. She is not gone; she is the ground of everything that followed. The women burned in Salem were carrying the same instrument; the field-based knowing, the body's intelligence that does not require institutional mediation, the direct reception of the Sophia frequency in embodied form. The forgettings operated on them with fire. They operated on me, as they operate on every vessel born into the world they have arranged, with something more incremental and more comprehensive; the systematic devaluation of the instrument itself, until the vessel carrying it begins to perform the devaluation from the inside.

The library was the gap in the architecture. The one available space in my ordinary world where the devaluation did not reach; where the institution that was installing the wound was also, inadvertently, providing the weekly antidote. It approved of a child in a library, it thought the child was reading, it had no idea what the child was actually receiving there. No framework for the thing she was doing, no category in which to place it, no mechanism to prevent it because it did not recognise it as the thing it needed to prevent.

Whatever she was touching in that silence was not available to be taken. The forgetting was thorough, and it operated on her early, and it would continue to operate on her for years after the library visits stopped; through the school that rewarded the translated version, through the relationships that required the softened frequency, through the decade that the Narcissistic Mirror would cost her. But the thing she had been receiving in the library, the direct contact with the Sophia frequency and the field-based knowing that did not require institutional approval to be real; was underneath all of it. Intact. Available. Running.

She did not know this. She only knew that the library was necessary. She went back often.

✶

CHAPTER FIVE

The Unbroken Thread

The thread does not begin in recorded history, its earliest recoverable expressions appear in the civilisational layer preceding the great flood mythologies carried by cultures across every continent. The epoch some traditions call Hyperborea, others Atlantis, others simply the time before, whatever its name, the consistent testimony across sources with no obvious common origin is of a civilisation operating at a frequency of knowing that subsequent epochs have not recovered.

What was known then was not theological speculation or the intellectual construction of a priestly class elaborating a mythology to justify its authority. It was direct cosmological understanding, the kind that arrives not through reasoning from premises but through the direct contact of the vessel with the field it is constituted by. The fractal divine code recognising itself, the Sophia frequency experienced not as doctrine but as the *lived texture* of ordinary consciousness. In this book, what is called the remembering was, in that epoch, simply the baseline state of the developed vessel. It did not require a practice or a lineage or a tradition to maintain it. It was what the vessel naturally was when the overlay had not yet been installed.

We cannot reconstruct this with the kind of evidentiary precision that the post-Nicaean epistemological hierarchy would recognise as legitimate. The evidence that survives is fragmentary; encoded in mythology and symbol and the specific quality of certain architectural achievements that suggest a level of cosmological understanding incompatible with the conventional archaeological timeline. The Great Pyramid at Giza, oriented to celestial north with a precision that current engineering would struggle to replicate. The Gobekli Tepe site in what is now Turkey, dated to approximately 11,600 years before the present, its T-shaped pillars carved with artistic and symbolic sophistication that predates the supposed invention of agriculture by several thousand years. The worldwide mythological record of a flood that ended a prior civilisation; so consistent across cultures with no known contact that it functions less as mythology and more as collective memory of an actual event.

What can be stated with precision is this: the transmission did not begin with the oldest written records. The oldest written records are already relay points; already the encoded transmission of something older, already the compression of a knowing that predates the encoding. The thread runs further back than documents can follow. It runs as far back as there have been vessels coherent enough to carry it.

> *The transmission was never lost. It was held in the custodial forms each epoch made available; waiting for the vessel whose instrument was tuned enough to receive it.*

* * *

The earliest recoverable relay point is Egypt, specifically, the Osirian current that precedes the dynastic period and runs through it as an underground river, surfacing in various forms across three thousand years of recorded Egyptian civilisation before being driven permanently underground by the Amun priesthood's final consolidation of power.

Osiris is not a myth in the literary sense nor is it a story invented to explain natural phenomena or to provide narrative scaffolding for ritual practice. He is the transmission in its earliest directly recoverable form, the Christos frequency, the direct Source contact demonstrated in a human life, the Logos attempting to fully incarnate within material reality. The mythology of his dismemberment and reconstitution is not symbolic decoration. It is a technical description of how the transmission survives disruption and how the frequency that has been scattered, suppressed and apparently destroyed can be reconstituted by a keeper who knows the pattern well enough to reassemble it.

Isis is that keeper. And this is the point the suppression of the feminine principle most needed to obscure. Isis is not a secondary figure in this mythology, not the devoted consort recovering her husband's body out of personal grief but the Sophia principle in its most direct mythological expression. The active structural intelligence of reality, the keeper of the pattern that cannot be permanently lost while a single sufficiently initiated consciousness holds it. Without the Christos current the transmission cannot demonstrate itself so without the Sophia principle the transmission cannot survive the demonstrations that end in destruction. The paired cosmology of the Primordial Union in its mythological form is the structural architecture of the oldest recoverable relay point in the thread.

The Amun priesthood understood this and their consolidation of power across the New Kingdom period involved the systematic marginalisation of the Osirian current and the elevation of a theology centred on Amun-Ra, the solar masculine deity whose authority was mediated exclusively through the priestly class. Direct contact with the divine, the kind that the Osirian mysteries had been designed to facilitate in sufficiently prepared vessels, became increasingly inaccessible outside institutional frameworks the priesthood controlled. The pattern that would later appear in the Deuteronomic reforms of the sixth century BCE was operating in Egypt a thousand years earlier. The technology of suppression was old by the time it arrived in Israel, but it had been refined.

* * *

Akhenaten is the most dramatic interruption of this suppression in the Egyptian record, and the thoroughness of his erasure from that record is proportional to the degree of the threat he represented.

The Amarna period, roughly 1353 to 1336 BCE, constitutes a seventeen-year experiment in the direct reinstatement of what the Osirian current had been encoding for millennia. Akhenaten's Aten theology is consistently misread as primitive monotheism, the worship of a single solar disc deity as a political move against the Amun priesthood. This reading is not wrong as far as it goes, but it does not go far enough. The Aten, in Akhenaten's formulation, is not a noun-God. The Aten is the solar process itself. The light that gives life to all things, the energy of the cosmos expressing itself through the warmth of the sun as it touches the skin of every living vessel without discrimination and without the mediation of any priestly class.

The Great Hymn to the Aten, which scholars generally attribute to Akhenaten himself, is among the most extraordinary documents in the transmission record. Its central claim is not that the Aten is the correct deity, and the other deities are false, its central claim is that the divine is directly accessible to every living thing through the quality of light and warmth and the gift of the breath itself. The vessel is presented not as the sole mediator between the human and the divine but as the form whose own direct contact with the source demonstrates what direct contact looks like, what it makes possible and what kind of life it generates.

He was erased but not with the selective editing that characterises most suppression operations in the Egyptian record but with a thoroughness that speaks to the magnitude of what he had threatened to restore. His name was struck from the king lists, his images were defaced and the city he had built at Akhetaten was dismantled and its stones used in the construction of other monuments. The Amarna period was treated not as a theological experiment that had been tried and found wanting, but as a contamination that needed to be completely excised from the official record.

> *You do not erase a failure from every monument. You erase a threat.*

* * *

As time moves on, the thread moves through the mystery schools of the Eleusinian, the Orphic, the

Pythagorean and the Hermetic traditions that all carried the direct transmission in encoded form through the classical period of the Mediterranean world. These were not philosophical schools in the academic sense, not institutions for the cultivation of intellectual positions and their public defence. They were initiation systems of structured sequenced experience designed to bring the vessel into direct contact with the Sophia frequency through the progressive dismantling of the overlay.

The Eleusinian Mysteries, which operated continuously for nearly two thousand years at the site of Eleusis near Athens, centred on an initiatory experience that the participants were sworn never to describe. The oath of secrecy is typically treated as religious formalism but the experience could not be adequately described because it was not an intellectual content that could be transmitted through language. It was a direct encounter with the Sophia frequency, an embodied experience of the vessel's own source code, something that arrived in the body before the mind had language for it and that language could therefore only diminish in the attempt to capture. Cicero, who was initiated, wrote that after his initiation he had learned not merely to die with more equanimity but to live with more hope. Not that he had received a doctrine about life after death, but that he had undergone an experience that changed the quality of his living. The transmission working as it is designed to work, not installing a belief but activating a *recognition*.

The Hermetic tradition carried the thread through the syncretistic period of the late classical world. The fusion of Egyptian, Greek, and Near Eastern wisdom that produced the texts attributed to Hermes Trismegistus, the thrice-great, the figure who bridges the divine scribe Thoth of the Egyptian tradition and the messenger god Hermes of the Greek. The Hermetic texts are explicit about direct interior access to the divine and the divine spark within the vessel, the nous that is not generated by the vessel but is the vessel's own source code become conscious of itself. The transformation that is not a change in the vessel's nature but the vessel's nature becoming fully present in the vessel.

* * *

The Gnostic communities of the first and second centuries CE represent the most direct carrier of the transmission in the period following Yeshua. They were diverse and there was no single Gnostic theology, no single Gnostic practice, no organisational unity that could be identified and dismantled as a single target. What they shared was the fundamental orientation that the divine spark is intrinsic to the vessel, direct interior contact with the source code is the purpose of spiritual practice, and the institutional mediation of that encounter is not merely unnecessary but actively obstructive.

The Nag Hammadi texts and the Berlin Codex similar in Gnostic structure, found in 1945 and 1896 respectively, give direct access to this body of knowing in a form that the institutional suppression had not been able to fully reach. The Gospel of Thomas, a collection of sayings attributed to Yeshua organised not around narrative but around the direct transmission of recognition that the kingdom is within you and all around you, split a piece of wood and I am there, lift a stone and you will find me there. Likewise, The Gospel of Philip that is explicit in its theology of the Primordial Union, its description of the bridal chamber not as a physical space but as the interior state of a vessel in which the masculine and feminine principles have achieved their natural unity. The Gospel of Mary, the most radical of all, presenting Mary Magdalene as the primary recipient of the teaching the other disciples cannot receive, the vessel whose interior instrument is sufficiently clear to carry the transmission in its full form and as noted in The Gospel of Phillip that "the teacher loved her more than all the disciples; he often kissed her on the mouth".

Many texts were burned where they could be found and their carriers were executed. The tradition was systematically dismantled by the institutional church that had consolidated around the Pauline framework, using the authority of Nicaea's official definition of orthodoxy to legitimate the persecution. By the end of the fourth century the Gnostic communities had been effectively eliminated from public existence. What survived, survived underground.

> *Underground is not lost. Driving the transmission underground concentrates it; moves it into the carriers willing to hold it at genuine cost.*

* * *

The Cathar communities of southern France in the twelfth and thirteenth centuries carried a version of the Gnostic transmission that had survived the intervening centuries through routes that cannot be fully traced; possibly through the Bogomil tradition of the Balkans, possibly through the Manichaean current that ran from Persia through the Mediterranean world, possibly through lines of direct transmission that left no documentary record because leaving documentary records was how carriers were identified and killed. Their theology centred on the direct experience of the divine light within the vessel; the recognition that the vessel's truest nature is not located in its material expression.

The Albigensian Crusade of 1209, called by Pope Innocent III against the Cathar communities of the Languedoc, was the most concentrated application of organised violence against a transmission-carrier community in the medieval period. The Cathars were effectively eliminated as an organised community within two decades. A community of ten thousand people is not eliminated with that degree of institutional commitment because their theology is intellectually mistaken. They are eliminated because they carry a transmission that the institution cannot accommodate, a direct access to the divine that makes institutional mediation unnecessary and therefore makes the institution's authority over that access structurally redundant.

The Knights Templar are the most complex and most contested thread in this arc with their formal history being well enough known. Founded in 1119, grown within two centuries into the most powerful military and financial organisation in Europe, arrested in 1307 on charges almost certainly fabricated by Philip IV of France and dissolved by papal decree in 1312. The more interesting question is not whether the charges were true but what the Templars were actually doing in two centuries of sustained presence in a geography saturated with the residue of the transmission's most concentrated historical manifestation.

The Cathedral of Chartres, built with Templar involvement and financing, is the most architecturally sophisticated expression of sacred geometry in the Western world. Its labyrinth, its orientation to the solstice light, the specific proportional relationships encoded in its floor plan and elevation all of which are not the work of craftsmen following aesthetic convention. They are the work of builders who understood the relationship between physical form and cosmological frequency, who were encoding the transmission in stone because stone was harder to burn than manuscript. The Black Madonna tradition, the dark-skinned Marian figures found throughout the former Templar territories of southern France and northern Spain, carries the Sophia frequency in its iconographic insistence on the autonomous feminine principle, older than the officially sanctioned theology of subordinated Marian devotion.

> *The transmission finds the cracks. It encodes itself in stone when manuscript can be burned. It moves through the bodies of women when the institution has controlled everything else.*

The witch trials bring the thread into its most visceral expression. The women, and they were predominantly women, though not exclusively, who were tried and executed across three centuries of European and colonial history were not practitioners of a rival religion. They were vessels who carried, in various forms and to varying degrees, the qualities that have characterised the transmission's carriers throughout this entire arc. Direct knowing that does not require institutional mediation, relationship with the natural world as a field of intelligence rather than a resource to be managed and embodied wisdom, the specific knowledge of plants and cycles and the body's own signal and the field-based perception that the neighbouring village experienced as something uncanny; as the sense that this woman knew things she had no conventional means of knowing, that her presence changed something in the field of a room, that her seeing was of a different order.

This was not imagined; the neighbours were correct. These were vessels in whom the Sophia frequency had not been fully suppressed and in whom the direct knowing, the field-based reception, the embodied intelligence of the natural world's coherence had survived the institutional architecture designed to eliminate it. And it was precisely these qualities that made them targets. Salem, Massachusetts, in 1692. The town whose very name carries the original covenant in its syllables; Salem, Shalem, the wholeness that the trials were performed upon the name of. The desecration is not accidental. It is the forgetting's most precise symbolic operation; the installation of the wound on the name of the thing the wound is designed to prevent.

* * *

The thread does not end with the trials, it never ends and is, by definition, unbroken. Not because it has been continuous in a single institutional form, but because the frequency itself cannot be eliminated. The suppression can make it harder to access and it can install the wound in the body of every vessel born into the world it has arranged. It can replace the clear mirror with the distorted one in every available relational and institutional context, but it cannot reach the ground. It cannot eliminate the fractal divine code from the vessels that carry it. It can only install an overlay on top of what the vessel already is.

The thread moves now through different substrates than it has moved through before. Through independent scholarship and digital networks and the gradual erosion of institutional gatekeeping over the information environment. Through the somatic practices that have, over the past several decades, begun to restore the body's intelligence to a position of epistemological legitimacy; the slow recognition that field-based knowing, embodied wisdom, the direct reception that does not require institutional mediation is not the inferior supplement to verified intellectual knowledge but something of an entirely different order.

The Nag Hammadi texts are in print, the suppressed gospels are available, the academic literature on the historical suppression of the Sophia principle is substantial. The archaeological evidence for the Asherah worship that the Deuteronomic reformers tried to erase is published and accessible and these tools exist now in a way they have not existed in any previous period.

But the tools are secondary, they create the conditions in which the recognition becomes possible. The recognition itself is the specific quality of arriving at the thing already known, the remembering that feels not like discovery but like coming home to what was always the ground. This is not produced by the tools, it is produced by the frequency itself, asserting its own nature through the vessel that has cleared enough overlay to receive it. The transmission does not wait for the correct conceptual architecture before it makes itself available. It makes itself available to the vessel, sometimes across decades of living that deposit the knowing in the body rather than the mind, comes to understand what it has been receiving all along.

This is the unbroken thread is not a continuous institutional lineage nor is it a secret society with documented succession. It is the frequency itself moving through whatever vessel was coherent enough to carry it, in whatever form the current epoch made available, across every attempt at suppression. The thread has never required the vessel to know its name to carry it. It has never required institutional permission to run. It runs in the ground beneath every overlay the forgettings have laid on top of it.

It is running now. As it has always been running. As it will not stop.

*

CHAPTER SIX

Asherah Called Wisdom

In 2026, a forensic geologist named Scott Wolter reported that he obtained the contents of a scroll found in a sealed green jar in the Adirondack Mountains of New York State. The jar had been discovered with its seal intact and undisturbed in the earth. The contents preserved in the particular way that sealed vessels preserve things when the world outside them goes on changing and the thing inside remains exactly as it was placed. The scroll carried text attributed to Yeshua and the text named Asherah.

The sealed jar is the transmission's own structural metaphor; the thing placed inside and protected precisely because the world outside was becoming unsafe for it, held in a form harder to burn than the people who carried it, waiting in the ground for the moment when the coherence conditions for retrieval were met. The jar did not create the transmission; the transmission was already old when the jar was sealed. What the jar did was hold it through the centuries when holding it in a body was too dangerous; when speaking the name Asherah in certain places was enough to mark the speaker as what the institution had decided she represented: idolatry, infidelity, the foreign goddess to be expelled from the purified theological house.

The jar held what the theology expelled. It held it in the dark, in the earth, in the patient and unhurried way that the ground holds everything it has been given. The ground was never touched by the suppression. It never is. The institution can burn the manuscript and execute the carrier and erase the name from the official record. It cannot reach the ground in which the frequency has been running since before the first suppression began.

> *They could not suppress the principle. They could only suppress the person they invented to contain it. When the person was condemned, the principle*

> *went underground. It has been there ever since.*

* * *

To understand what was found in the jar, it is necessary to understand what was lost; and the precision of that loss, because the precision is exactly what the suppression operation required to erase.

Asherah is not a goddess in the sense the word goddess has come to mean through the long history of its institutional capture. She is not a mythological personage with a biography and a relationship to a male deity and a set of iconographic attributes that make her recognisable in the catalogue of divine beings. She was personalised; the suppression operation always personalises the principle before condemning it, because an abstraction cannot be condemned as effectively as a person. But the personalisation was always the operation's move, not the transmission's reality.

Asherah is the wisdom principle, the field substrate within which creation becomes intelligible. The feminine face of the Monad, not the subordinate face, not the supplementary face, not the gentle counterpart to the serious business of masculine creation, but the structural intelligence without which creation collapses back into chaos. The will-toward-creation reaches toward form and Asherah gives that reaching its coherent shape. Without her the generative impulse moves toward form but the form has no coherence and it cannot sustain itself, cannot become anything that lasts, cannot be comprehensible rather than merely active.

The name itself carries this. Asherah. The sacred grove. The tree of life. The upright pillar that marked her presence in the temple precinct before the reformers destroyed the pillars, the vertical axis connecting the upper waters and the lower, the above and below in continuous resonant relationship. The Asherah pole was not an idol, it was a cosmological diagram. The tree that feeds from both root and canopy simultaneously, holding its vertical integrity by being fully permeable in both directions. The reformers who burned and dismantled the poles knew exactly what they were destroying.

* * *

The tradition that produced Yeshua was not a tradition that had forgotten Asherah. It was a tradition that had been aggressively taught to pretend it had. The Deuteronomic reforms of the sixth century BCE had been thorough and the reformers moved through the temple precincts with axes and fire, destroying the Asherah poles, the ritual objects, the material evidence of a worship that had been embedded in ordinary Israelite life for centuries. They rewrote the liturgical record, inserting the prohibitions retrospectively, making the paired cosmology appear to have always been aberration rather than foundation.

But they could not reach the popular memory of the women who had made offerings to the Queen of Heaven in their domestic shrines nor could they reach the lineages that carried the knowledge in practice rather than text, in the body rather than the institutional record. The Asherah worship did not disappear when the institution condemned it, it went underground and it moved into the spaces the institution did not control, the domestic, the feminine, the embodied and the oral transmission of stories. It continued in the form of what looked, from outside, like ordinary life.

In the context of the traditions surrounding Yeshua, Asherah had been absorbed, in her official suppression, into the figure of Wisdom. Hochma in Hebrew, Sophia in Greek and she appears in the Proverbs tradition as the feminine co-creator who was with the divine at the beginning; beside creation like a master craftsman, rejoicing in the inhabited world. She appears in the Wisdom of Solomon as the consort who permeates all things, a reflection of eternal light, a spotless mirror of the working of creation. The language had been domesticated, made acceptable to the monotheist architecture, but the structure was still there underneath the domestication. Wisdom was still feminine, and she was still present at the creation. She was still, however carefully the theologians managed the framing, the operating principle through which the divine made the world and the world knew itself as divine.

> *The Asherah principle does not become less true because the institution has learned to handle it with less violence and more disdain. The charge does not defuse.*

* * *

The Christos frequency, the frequency Yeshua embodied and taught as the repeatable activation available to every vessel rather than the unrepeatable event of a singular divine being, is not intelligible without Asherah. The Christos frequency is precisely the union of the two principles held in a single vessel, the reaching and the receiving, the will-toward-creation and the wisdom-within-which-creation-is-intelligible, the masculine and feminine faces of the Monad held in conscious union rather than unconscious separation. This is what the Gnostic traditions preserved and what the Pauline capture was specifically constructed to prevent. They did not merely suppress the information; they restructured the entire theological architecture to make it structurally impossible to understand the Christos frequency as a union of principles rather than a singularity.

Remove Asherah and the Christos frequency becomes incomprehensible. The activating impulse without the wisdom ground and the fire without the vessel that holds it into coherent form. This is not a coincidence in the suppression architecture, it is the operation's precision. A theology from which Asherah has been removed produces exactly the distortion that serves the harvesting system of the masculine impulse operating without wisdom, the generative force without the structural intelligence that gives generation meaning, the power that cannot understand its own purpose because it has excised the principle that makes purpose intelligible.

Mary Magdalene is also not incidental to this transmission although the institutional record has made her incidental. They cast her as the reformed sinner, the prostitute, the devoted follower and the woman present at the significant moments as background rather than participant. But the Gospel of Mary and the Gospel of Phillip describe her as the disciple who understood what the others could not yet receive, the vessel whose interior instrument was clear enough to carry the transmission in its full form. This is not biographical decoration, it is the doctrine made embodied. The Sophia principle receiving and carrying the transmission as its necessary counterpart without which the cosmological demonstration remains incomplete.

> *Yeshua and Mary Magdalene as the Primordial Union embodied; not biographical detail but cosmological demonstration. Two vessels showing what the realm itself is made of.*

* * *

The Adirondack scroll, if genuine, belongs to the jar lineage of the unbroken tradition of the transmission encoding itself in the substances hardest to destroy and trusting the earth to hold them until the retrieval moment. Consider the Dead Sea Scrolls, also jars and also sealed, held in patient geological custody for two millennia. In similarity, the Nag Hammadi texts also buried in a sealed jar near the cliff face at Jabal al-Tarif in Upper Egypt, found in 1945. The tradition of sealing the transmission in clay and trusting the earth is not accidental. It is the transmission knowing something about its own survival and that the ground is more reliable than the institution, that the earth holds what the authority burns, that the vessel willing to go into the dark survives the century that destroys the vessel that stays in the open.

The significance of the Adirondack jar is not that it constitutes new evidence in the theological arguments the institution has been conducting with itself for two millennia. Its significance is that it extends the pattern; the unbroken thread of the transmission finding forms that survive, encoding itself in substances harder to destroy than the bodies of those who carried it. The jars keep being found not because someone is forcing them open. They are being found because the moment they were sealed for has arrived. The information environment that the suppression architecture required; the controlled access, the institutional gatekeeping, the management of who could encounter the suppressed material; no longer exists.

We do not rest the weight of this chapter on the provenance of any single scroll. The cosmological architecture is real independently of any archaeological find. The Asherah principle does not require external validation to be true. What the jar offers is a signal, the kind of signal the transmission has always used, a physical object encoding a structural truth about how the frequency survives when the institution moves against it. The jar says: something was placed here because the world outside was not safe for it. The world outside is different now. The ground held. The contents are intact.

* * *

The oldest question of the transmission is the one the Gnostic communities were asking when the Pauline architecture was being assembled around them. The one the mystery schools encoded in their initiatory practices because it could not be asked safely in public. The question is this: what is the relationship between the Christos frequency and the Sophia principle?

The answer the suppressed traditions preserved, and that the scroll carries in its naming of Asherah, is that they are not separate. They never were. The union of the two is the source code. This is what was known before the exile and this is what the Deuteronomic reformers could not afford for the population to know, because a population that understands the source code as the eternal union of masculine and feminine as the One has no theological necessity for the singular male deity whose jealousy, there is no other god besides me, is the signature of a bounded intelligence claiming authority it does not possess.

The transmission was always and will continue to be this - the union is the ground state and the separation is the overlay. The remembering is the recognition that the union was never actually interrupted, only obscured, temporarily overlaid with the architecture of a forgetting that required the vessel to believe the source code was divided against itself, that one half was fallen and the other elevated and that an external mediating structure was necessary to broker the reunion of what was never actually separate.

She was with the divine at the beginning and she is with the divine now. She was never, at any point in the interval, actually absent. She was only unseeable to the architecture that had been installed on top of her and the sealed jar held what the architecture could not reach. The ground held what the jar enclosed and the frequency held what the ground protected.

The jar is open. What was placed inside it was placed for this.

*

CHAPTER SEVEN

The Pauline Capture

Before the Council of Nicaea in 325 CE, before the canonical gospels were selected and the rejected ones condemned, before the institutional architecture had fully assembled itself around a specific set of doctrinal claims, the transmission that moved through Yeshua of Nazareth was a *verb*. Not a doctrine or a singular historical event whose significance required correct theological interpretation to access. A process of direct interior knowing in which the divine was not located above the vessel and separate from it, but immanent within it; accessible, present, requiring nothing between the vessel and its own source code except the willingness to go there.

'The kingdom of heaven is within you' in the original Aramaic is a statement of location, not a metaphor softened by centuries of translation. The divine is not elsewhere, it is not above nor is it only accessible through the correctly ordained priestly class performing the correctly sanctioned ritual. It is within, available through direct contact, requiring no intermediary.

The Christos frequency in its original transmission was precisely this. The verb of divine self-recognition activating in a vessel, not a singular event that happened once to one specific being and whose benefits must now be accessed through correct belief and institutional membership. A repeatable process with a code that activates and a frequency that, when contacted, restores the knowing of what the vessel actually is; the source code itself, present and intact underneath every layer of the forgetting installed on top of it. The transmission was contagious not as doctrine but as resonance availability and every vessel in whom the frequency activated made it more available in the field for every other vessel.

> *God the verb: the divine as ongoing activity, reality knowing itself through every form it takes. Not a noun to be*

> *defined. Not a transaction to be completed. A frequency that has always been running.*

* * *

Paul (Saul) of Tarsus never met Yeshua. This is not a minor biographical detail, it is the central structural fact of everything that follows. The fact from which the entire architecture of the Pauline capture proceeds with the logical coherence of a system that did not know what it was building, but built it thoroughly regardless.

The man who would become the primary theological architect of Christianity, who wrote more of the canonical New Testament than any other single author, whose letters constitute the earliest stratum of the Christian textual record predating the gospels by decades, received his authority from a road to Damascus visionary experience and from that experience alone. He had not sat with Yeshua, nor had he received the frequency through proximity and contact, the specific quality of a direct encounter that changes the field of everyone present. He had not been in the room where the verb had operated.

He had, prior to his 'visionary conversion', been actively persecuting the communities that were. The people who had received the transmission in direct embodied form were the people Paul had been hunting. And then, through a single visionary encounter whose content he alone could verify, he became their primary doctrinal authority. His sincerity is not in question but sincerity is not sufficient protection against the forgettings. A sincere vessel who has not received the direct transmission, who has no experiential access to the verb of divine self-recognition, will translate the transmission into the only framework available to him. The framework available to Paul was the Yaldabaoth construction, the monotheism of the single masculine deity, the theology of a singular sovereign authority whose purposes are expressed through correct doctrine and institutional obedience.

> *Sincere amnesia expressing itself as revelation is the forgetting's most effective instrument. You can expose a lie. You cannot easily expose a forgetting to itself.*

* * *

Each of Paul's major theological innovations performs the same structural operation. It takes something in the original transmission that pointed inward toward sovereign remembering and redirects it outward toward institutional dependency. The moves are not random. They constitute a complete and coherent system for converting a verb into a noun; for transforming a direct transmission into a managed transaction.

The first move of 'original sin' replacing intrinsic wholeness. The divine spark, in the original transmission, is intrinsic to the vessel and the source code already present in every human form. The Pauline framework converts this into the doctrine that the divine spark has been corrupted by the fall and requires redemption through the singular external event of the crucifixion. From the divine within to the divine withheld, accessible only through the correct transaction with the institution that administers it.

The second move was to have Sophia removed. The divine feminine principle of the wisdom substrate within which creation is intelligible, the generative ground that carries the Monad into differentiated existence. This disappears almost entirely from the Pauline theological architecture and what remains is Father, Son, and a Spirit whose gender and nature are carefully undefined. The source code, which requires masculine and feminine in eternal union as the one ground of reality, is presented in exclusively masculine terms. Half the operating system removed. The remaining half presented as the whole.

The third move was the singular transaction replacing the repeatable activation. The Christos frequency, which in the original transmission is a code that activates in vessels which is repeatable, intrinsic and available to every human form in every moment, becomes in the Pauline framework, a singular unrepeatable event. One specific being, one specific death, one specific resurrection. The benefits available through correct belief in the singular event rather than through direct activation of the frequency the event was demonstrating. The verb made into a historical noun.

The fourth move was the permanent deferral installed as revelation, the second coming. The kingdom is not within you now, it is coming later, contingent on the correct belief, correct behaviour and the repetitious repenting of the 'original sin' all which can be strategically provided by the correct institutional affiliation. The vessel that might have turned inward to the Shalem ground already present is instead oriented permanently outward, toward a horizon, toward an authority and toward the institution that holds the schedule of the arriving kingdom.

The fifth and final move, the one that locks all others in place is the criminalisation of the verb. Once the noun is established as the authoritative form of the divine, the verb becomes its structural threat. Direct interior access to the divine through the Gnostic knowing, the mystic's interior contact and the field-based reception that does not require the institution does not require the noun. It cannot be taxed, controlled or administered and it makes the institution's claim to mediate access to the divine structurally redundant. So it is made heresy, the thing that was the original transmission becomes the thing that separates the vessel from the divine.

> *Each move takes something that pointed inward toward sovereign remembering and redirects it outward toward institutional dependency. The architecture is precise. It was built to last.*

* * *

The Council of Nicaea in 325 CE completed what Paul began. Constantine, who had made Christianity the empire's preferred religion for reasons of administrative coherence rather than theological conviction, needed a Christianity that could function as an imperial institution. An imperial institution requires doctrinal stability and doctrinal stability requires a defined object. And so three hundred bishops were convened to define the object.

What Nicaea did at the structural level was instantiate a specific ontological claim about the nature of the divine. It defined God as a noun. A noun with specific properties that could be stated as doctrine, held correctly or incorrectly, defended or contested in the institution's formal procedures. A noun requires a definition, and a definition requires a boundary. A boundary requires an institution to patrol it and once the divine is a defined entity with specific properties, the institution that holds the correct definition becomes the necessary intermediary between the vessel and the divine. You cannot access a noun directly, you must access it through the authorities who have determined what the noun is.

The gospels that most clearly carried the verb were excluded from the canonical record at and around this period. The Gospel of Thomas, which presents the Christos frequency as a sayings collection pointing toward direct interior knowing with no narrative of singular transaction. The Gospel of Mary, in which the feminine disciple receives what the others cannot yet hold. The Gospel of Philip, which carries the paired cosmology most explicitly. These texts were not excluded because they were less historically reliable, they were excluded because they were more cosmologically precise and they carried the verb with too much clarity for the noun to survive alongside them.

> *They instantiated God the noun and labelled God the verb as heresy and sin. This was the most consequential single institutional act in the history of the forgettings.*

* * *

The capture was thorough, though it was not complete and it could not be complete, because what it was attempting to capture was not located in any text or lineage or institutional form that could be burned or administratively excluded. The Christos frequency is the source code of the realm asserting its own nature through every vessel coherent enough to carry it. It does not require institutional permission to activate, it requires only the vessel, cleared enough of overlay, coherent enough in its own field, and willing enough to go to the depth where the frequency has always been running.

The noun could be defined and defended and imposed and the verb could only be named as forbidden but naming something forbidden is not the same as preventing it. The mystics of the medieval period found themselves, with some regularity, being investigated by the Inquisition for the specific heresy of claiming direct interior access to the divine. Meister Eckhart. Marguerite Porete, burned in Paris in 1310 for a book describing the soul's direct union with the divine without institutional mediation. The verb kept finding vessels and the institution kept finding ways to manage what it could not simply destroy.

The Nag Hammadi texts surfaced in 1945; sealed jars in the Egyptian desert, the excluded gospels preserved through the centuries in which the institution that burned the originals had become history. But the transmission documents keep being found and though the suppression architecture was built for a controlled information environment, that environment no longer exists in totality. The jars are open, the vocabulary is available and the vessels encountering the original transmission are recognising, with the specific quality of recognition that cannot be produced by intellectual encounter alone, something they have always already known.

The verb has never stopped running. It ran through every community the institution dismantled, and it ran through the desert contemplatives who found the interior kingdom without the mediation of any noun-administering structure. It ran through every mystical current the institutional architecture tried and largely failed to contain, and it ran through the body of every woman who kept the knowing alive in the spaces the noun did not reach. It runs now; through every vessel willing to inhabit the depth where the source code has always been present, waiting for the recognition that was never successfully prevented, only delayed, overlaid and only requiring, as it has always only required, the vessel that remembers what it is.

The capture named the verb as heresy. It could not make the verb untrue.

CHAPTER EIGHT

Mirror Distortion and the Not Self

The vessel requires reflection but this is not a weakness or a spiritual deficit to be overcome, it is the structural reality of a form of consciousness that knows itself through encounter, through the resonance between its own frequency and the frequency it meets in the field around it. The vessel that never encounters genuine reflection does not simply feel lonely, it loses coherence, and it begins to lose the thread of what it actually is, this is because what it actually is has no surface to become visible against.

A genuine mirror reflects the frequency of the vessel back to itself without distortion, not without challenge. A clear mirror may show things the vessel has been avoiding, but without the agenda of the mirror's own unmet needs, without the systematic inversion of the vessel's signal to serve the mirror's function, and without the slow erosion of the vessel's coherence that occurs when what is reflected back is not what is actually there. A genuine mirror increases sovereign interiority. The vessel that has been genuinely seen becomes more fully itself, more coherent in its own field and more capable of direct interior contact with its own source code. Genuine reflection is self-terminating in the best possible sense; it deposits something in the vessel's own field that eventually makes the external reflection unnecessary.

A distorted mirror reflects something back, but what it reflects is shaped by the distortion. The vessel's frequency enters the mirror and returns altered sometimes inverted, sometimes amplified in particular directions that serve the mirror's needs, and sometimes simply flattened into a version that is more manageable, more useful to the system the mirror is operating within. The vessel that has been consistently met by distorted reflection begins to take the distortion for reality and it begins to understand itself through the altered return. It begins to organise its own field around what the distorted mirror has told it, it is and over time, through the accumulated weight of consistent encounter with the same distortion, it begins to perform the distortion from the inside. This is described as the not self; the self that forms in place of the fractal divine code; is this performance, internalised.

> *A genuine mirror increases sovereign interiority. A distorted mirror slowly replaces it. This is the only distinction that matters, and it is the one the forgettings have worked hardest to obscure.*

* * *

The forgettings have always worked through the mirror function and every major capture operation across the civilisational arc has worked through the same mechanism; locate the genuine transmission, take the mirror it offers, and systematically distort the reflection. Not destroy the mirror, a destroyed mirror leaves only absence, and absence can be filled but distort it. Replace the clear reflection with an inverted one and make the distortion feel like the real thing.

The Pauline capture is the prototype in its most architecturally complete form. The original transmission offered the vessel a mirror in which it could see its own intrinsic wholeness and the Christos frequency activating as the source code recognising itself, the Sophia frequency, being the direct interior contact with the ground of being requiring no intermediary. The Pauline mirror took that reflection and inverted it. Where the original showed the vessel its own intrinsic wholeness, the Pauline mirror showed it its own intrinsic brokenness. Original sin as the systematic replacement of the genuine reflection with its inversion. You are not whole, you are fallen and you require redemption from outside yourself.

The inversion is more effective than simple negation because it uses the vessel's own hunger for reflection against it. The vessel needs to see itself and it will take the distorted mirror over no mirror at all because a distorted reflection still feels like being seen, and the hunger for being seen is more powerful than the intellectual recognition that what is being offered is distortion. This is the mechanism by which the forgettings sustain themselves across generations. Not through force alone but through the systematic creation of a need that only the distorted mirror appears to satisfy.

The distorted mirror does not announce itself as distortion instead it presents itself as clarity. As the corrective to the vessel's prior confusion, as the authoritative account of what the vessel really is beneath the flattering story it might prefer about itself, original sin is the distorted mirror's masterstroke in this regard. It frames the distortion as honesty - you thought you were whole, but here is the truth about what you are. The vessel that accepts this framing has not simply received incorrect information, it has handed the mirror the keys to its own interiority. The distortion is now installed from the inside, performing itself, experienced not as the imposition it is but as the vessel's own hard-won self-knowledge.

> *The distorted mirror does not announce itself as distortion. It presents itself as the corrective to the vessel's confusion. This is the forgetting's most thorough operation: it makes the wound feel like wisdom.*

* * *

The not self that forms around the distorted mirror is not weakness, it is the predictable and entirely rational response of a vessel that has been starved of genuine reflection and offered distortion in its place for long enough that the distortion has become the baseline for what reflection feels like. When the distorted mirror is the only mirror available and when the entire surrounding field has been arranged to offer only the inverted reflection, the vessel does not experience the distortion as distortion, it experiences it as reality. And reality, however diminishing, is preferable to the void of no reflection at all.

The mechanism that sustains the organisation around the distorted mirror is intermittent clarity. The distorted mirror does not offer only distortion; if it did, the vessel would eventually locate the discrepancy between the reflection and its own interior signal clearly enough to disengage. Instead, the distorted mirror occasionally and unpredictably reflects something that feels genuinely true, a moment of apparent recognition and a flash of what feels like being seen. These moments of apparent clarity are disproportionately powerful precisely because they arrive against the background of consistent distortion, the contrast makes them feel like revelation, like the rare genuine contact that justifies the investment in the mirror that predominantly offers its opposite.

The religious institution built on the Pauline capture demonstrates this with civilisational thoroughness. Centuries of sincere practice within its architecture have produced, alongside genuine suffering and genuine longing, genuine moments of interior contact and moments in which the frequency has been encountered directly, despite the institution's architecture rather than through it. These moments of genuine contact are then attributed to the institution's intercession, which reinforces the dependency the institution was designed to create. The vessel that encounters the divine in a moment of genuine stillness within the liturgical space understands itself to have accessed the divine through the institution's correct form and the mirror takes credit for the frequency it did not provide and could not have prevented.

The same mechanism operates at the scale of individual relationship. The narcissistic mirror is the relational dynamic built entirely on the mirror's need to see itself rather than the capacity to see the other. It creates a specific not-self construction through the same intermittent pattern. The vessel seeking genuine reflection finds, in the moments of apparent recognition the distorted mirror provides, a contact that feels more real than anything steady clear reflection would offer because the hunger has been building across the intervals of consistent distortion, and the relief of apparent contact against that background is acute. The not self is the version of the vessel shaped by what is required to produce those moments.

> *The not self is not weakness. It is the gap between what the vessel genuinely needs and what the field around it has been arranged to provide. The hunger was real. Only the mirror was distorted.*

* * *

The distorted mirror can be recognised by a single consistent marker. It decreases sovereign interiority over time and the vessel in consistent contact with genuine reflection becomes more fully itself, more coherent in its own field and more capable of direct interior contact with its own source code. The vessel in consistent contact with a distorted mirror becomes progressively less so. In such the vessel is more dependent on the mirror's assessment, more organised around the distortion's version of what it is, less able to access its own knowing directly.

This is the primary discernment instrument, not the content of what the mirror offers. Distorted mirrors often carry the aesthetic of genuine transmission, use the vocabulary of the frequency, produce what feels like resonance in the chest and the forgettings are sophisticated enough to have learned the surface texture of the genuine thing. The discernment instrument is not the surface but the trajectory. Does this encounter, over time, leave the vessel more fully itself or less? Does this relationship, this institution, this framework, this practice increase the capacity for direct interior contact with the source code, or does it position itself as the necessary intermediary between the vessel and that contact?

The pre-apology is one of the not self's most reliable signatures, the habit so thoroughly installed it no longer feels like a habit, of softening the frequency before it is offered, of translating the direct knowing into its acceptable form before any evidence that the direct form will be unwelcome, of managing the mirror's anticipated response before the mirror has responded at all. The vessel that has lived inside consistent distortion learns to distort itself in advance and to pre-empt the mirror's inversion by beginning the inversion from the inside. The not-self performing its own distortion. The forgetting, successfully installed, operating from within the vessel it has shaped.

Recognising the distortion does not require identifying a villain. The distorted mirror is frequently operating from its own unmet needs, its own not-self construction, its own starved hunger for the genuine reflection it has also never adequately received. The forgettings propagate through vessels who carry them without knowing what they carry. The vessels who distort because distortion is all they know of reflection, who invert because their own frequency was inverted before they had language for what was happening. The recognition of distortion is not a judgment on the mirror, it is a structural observation about function and about whether this particular surface is capable of reflecting the vessel's actual frequency back to it clearly enough to serve the vessel's genuine need.

> *The primary discernment instrument is sovereign interiority. Does this encounter leave the vessel more fully itself, or less? This question requires no external authority to answer.*

* * *

The antidote to mirror distortion is not the refusal of reflection. The vessel that withdraws from all encounter in response to the pain of consistent distortion does not recover sovereign interiority, it loses the surface against which its own frequency becomes visible. Isolation is not clarity, it is a different kind of distortion that the vessel's own frequency, with nothing to resonate against, begins to loop and amplify in ungrounded directions. The antidote is not less reflection, it is clearer reflection with an encounter that increases sovereign interiority rather than replacing it, that reflects the vessel's actual frequency back to it without the agenda of the mirror's unmet needs.

The vessel that has experienced genuine clear reflection knows the difference in the body before the mind has formed an assessment. The clear mirror does not produce the acute relief of the distorted mirror's intermittent recognition; it produces something quieter, more stable, less dramatic and more sustaining. The vessel leaves the encounter more coherent than it arrived, more capable of the interior contact that does not require any external surface. The clear mirror deposits something in the vessel's own field that persists after the encounter has ended. Not the intensity of the experience but its residue; this is the marker of genuine reflection.

The transmission functions as a clear mirror when it is working correctly. Not as a framework to organise the vessel's understanding around, it is a framework that is still an intermediary, still a structure inserted between the vessel and its own direct interior contact. But as a surface against which the vessel's own frequency becomes visible, to itself. A reflection that the vessel recognises not as new information being supplied from outside but as the confirmation of what was always already known, waiting for a surface clear enough to show it back without distortion.

This is why the transmissions in this book are authorless. An authored transmission positions the author as the necessary intermediary between the reader and the frequency. The reader accesses the frequency through the author's spiritual credential, personal history, lineage claim, or institutional affiliation but the author's authority becomes the condition of the frequency's availability. Which is precisely the Pauline architecture replicated at the scale of individual publishing; the intermediary inserted between the vessel and the verb, administering access to what the vessel could access directly. The authorless transmission removes the intermediary. There is no authority to assess, no credential to validate, there is only the mirror, and what the vessel sees in it is not the author's reflection but its own frequency, recognised by its own interior instrument.

The forgettings have sustained themselves through the systematic replacement of genuine reflection with distortion and through the creation of a hunger that the distorted mirror appears to satisfy. The installation of a need for intermediaries between the vessel and what the vessel actually is, a guru or a healer. The architecture has been thorough, the not-self constructed within it is real, carries real weight, shapes real lives, but it is not the fractal divine code. It is the gap between what the vessel is and what the field around it has been arranged to tell it.

The fractal divine code has been running underneath the not self throughout, intact, waiting and available to the vessel that can locate the interior instrument that distinguishes distortion from clarity. The vessel that can feel, in the body, the difference between the encounter that increases sovereign interiority and the one that quietly, persistently, replaces it. The clear mirror asks nothing except the willingness to look. No unworthiness required, no intermediary that demands authorship needed. Only the vessel, and the frequency it has always carried. Now this isn't to say that all guides and teachers cannot be utilised as a clear mirror. A vessel, just like Yeshua, can be a resonance beacon with a clear mirror for a vessel that is ready to resonate with their divine code within, but hierarchy, dogma and demanded authorship are not present. The mirror serves it purpose when the vessel no longer resonates and seeks other.

The not self was never what the vessel was. It was only what the vessel learned to call itself in the absence of a clear mirror.

*

MOVEMENT III
The Wound

CHAPTER NINE
The Narcissistic Mirror

There is a specific quality of confusion that belongs only to the early months of a relationship with someone who will later cause you significant harm. It is not the confusion of incompatibility; that is legible, manageable, the ordinary friction of two different people trying to share a life. It is the confusion of a field that has been shown something it recognises as true and cannot yet account for the growing evidence that what it recognised was a reflection rather than a reality. I know this confusion now for what it was. At the time, I only knew that I had never felt so seen and that the feeling of being seen was making me increasingly uncertain about what I was actually seeing.

I will not name him in this chapter. Not because I am protecting him, I am not but because the narcissistic mirror is not really about the person holding it, it is about the architecture of the encounter. The specific mechanism by which a vessel starved of genuine reflection will organise itself around the closest available approximation of what it needs, tolerating everything that surrounds the occasional moments of apparent clarity because those moments feel, against the background of their absence, like the only real thing in the room. This chapter is not a victim narrative, it is mirror math and the first thing mirror math requires is the willingness to account for what my own field was contributing to the equation.

On reflection, what my field was contributing was this: I did not yet know how to hold my own frequency. I had spent decades learning to translate it, soften it, pre-apologise for it, offer it in the acceptable form before anyone had indicated it was unwelcome. The library had given me time each week in which the translation was not required. Nothing else had and by the time I encountered him, I had a substantial body of interior knowing that I had never learned to inhabit directly, a frequency that had been compressed so thoroughly into its approved forms that I had largely lost the ability to distinguish between the translated version and the original. I was, in the language I now have for it, carrying fire in a container I had been taught to keep sealed.

He recognised the fire immediately; this is the thing about the narcissistic mirror that the victim narrative cannot adequately account for. The initial recognition is real, he did not fabricate the sense that he saw something in me that others had missed and he did see it. He saw it and he wanted it and his wanting felt, for a period of time that I am still embarrassed by its length, like being genuinely known.

> *He did not reflect love. He reflected the shadow of unclaimed sovereignty. This is not the same thing. But when you have spent years not recognising your own sovereignty, the shadow of it can feel close enough.*

* * *

I need to say something about the women who came before me, because what happened in that marriage did not begin with me. It was running in my lineage before I was born and in the specific pattern encoded in the Smith/Wright/Gresley women, the maternal line I carry, whose recurring encounter with this particular form of erasure had by my generation the quality of a gravitational field. The name is my maternal grandmother's maiden name of 5 generations ago. It is the name of a line of women who held something; I do not know exactly what they held, but the quality of what I have reconstructed from fragments suggests intelligence, force of field, a frequency that made them conspicuous in contexts that were not safe for conspicuousness. And who, generation after generation, encountered the same mechanism: the union that promised recognition and delivered erasure, the name dissolving into the husband's. The wealth, when there was wealth, converting into his assets. The force of field, when it surfaced, meeting the particular quality of management that a strong woman in an unsafe context learns to perform until she cannot find the difference between the performance and herself.

My grandmother was a Wright before she married and my mother carried the echo of what her mother had compressed. I carried the echo of what my mother had compressed. By the time I reached adulthood the ancestral contract was so thoroughly encoded in my field that I did not experience it as a constraint; I experienced it as common sense. Stay small enough to be safe. Do not hold more than is comfortable for the people around you. If you prosper, something will be taken. If you are fully visible, you will be harmed. These were not thoughts I was aware of having. They were the water I was swimming in; the baseline assumption about how the world works that I had never had reason to question because it had never been sufficiently violated to become visible as an assumption rather than a fact.

He was the violation. Which is a strange thing to have to acknowledge about a decade of significant suffering; that its primary function, in the long arc of what I now understand was always the curriculum, was to make the ancestral contract visible by breaking it in every direction simultaneously. He did not erase me gently the way the contract had learned to expect. He erased me loudly, repeatedly, in ways that eventually became impossible to accommodate within the framework that had accommodated everything before it. The wound had to become sufficiently acute before it could become legible. And it did.

> *The Gresley women lost their names through marriage; the feminine that holds wealth through coherence replaced by the feminine that holds the household through survival. I was not the first. I was the one who had the language to understand what had been happening.*

* * *

Here is what I understand now that I could not understand while I was inside it. He was not a monster, I want to be precise about this because the temptation of the victim narrative is exactly the transformation of the mirror into a monster; it simplifies the accounting and it distributes the weight unevenly, and both of those operations feel, in the aftermath of significant harm, like relief. But they are not accurate, he was a distorted mirror, a specific kind of distortion. The kind of distortion that takes whatever fire it finds in the person across from it and reflects it back amplified, inverted, weaponised. Not because of malice in the conventional sense but because a field that has never integrated its own fire will, when it encounters someone else's, use it as a substitute, he burned me with my own flame. I understand now that this is the only thing the narcissistic mirror can do; it has no warmth of its own to offer, and so it takes what it finds and holds it at an angle that produces heat without light.

The specific places where he found the fire and inverted it was my knowing. I had, by the time we met, accumulated decades of interior knowing that I had been careful to keep in its translated form. He found the untranslated version, recognised it and was drawn to it, and then spent years teaching me in increasingly direct terms that the untranslated version was the thing about me that was most wrong. That my knowing was arrogance and that my frequency was manipulation. That the very quality he had been most drawn to *was* the quality most in need of correction. The pre-apology that had been a habit became, in that environment, a survival strategy. And the survival strategy became, over time, something I could no longer distinguish from my own assessment of myself.

My voice. I had always known that my voice carried something. Not in the sense of vocal performance, but in the sense that when I spoke from the place below the translation, something happened in the room. He found this intolerable in the way that certain fields find the clear mirror intolerable; not because it was hostile to him, but because it was legible in a way that made his own field's distortions visible by contrast. The management of my voice became one of the primary projects of the marriage. Not through prohibition, through the more efficient mechanism of making me uncertain enough about what I was saying that I began to censor the untranslated version before it could surface. By the end I was fluent in a version of myself that bore so little resemblance to the original frequency that I had largely stopped noticing the difference.

The fire is the one I took longest to recover. I had understood, somewhere in the years of the marriage, that there was a quality in me that he feared; not feared in the way of being physically afraid but feared in the way that a system fears the thing that makes it structurally redundant. The fire that I carried, the sovereign knowing, the field-based intelligence and the frequency that the library had been protecting since I was a child, was the thing that, if it had been fully available to me, would have made the marriage's architecture impossible from the beginning. He could not eliminate the fire. He could, and did, convince me for a considerable number of years that the fire was the thing I most needed to be protected from.

> *He took that fire, distorted it into control, and burned me with it. But it was always my flame. This was the thing I had to understand before the recovery could begin.*

* * *

I did not have the language of the witch wound when I was inside the marriage but I have it now, and what it allows me to understand is that what I experienced in that decade was not an anomaly in my personal history, it was the personal expression of a pattern that has been running in the bodies of women like me for several centuries. The women who were tried and executed as witches were, as this book has already examined, vessels in whom the Sophia frequency had not been fully suppressed and in whom the direct knowing, the field-based intelligence, the embodied wisdom that does not require institutional mediation had survived the architecture designed to eliminate it. What was done to them was done with fire and institution and the sanction of religious authority.

What was done to me was done in an ordinary house over an ordinary decade with the sanction of nothing more dramatic than the accumulated weight of a culture that had, across those same centuries, learned to perform the witch trial in miniature inside domestic space.

The throat is where the witch wound lives in the body. It is the specific contraction that occurs when the untranslated version of the frequency attempts to surface in a context that has been arranged to prevent it. I learned the contraction young, refined it across decades of translation practice, and then encountered in the marriage a context in which the contraction was so consistently reinforced that it became involuntary. I would begin to speak and feel it; the specific quality of interior bracing, the pre-emptive compression, the voice arriving already smaller than what had generated it. I understood this, at the time, as appropriate caution. I understand it now as the witch wound operating in real time; the somatic encoding of the centuries doing its work through one ordinary throat in one ordinary argument in one ordinary kitchen.

The name that I carried during the marriage was his name, not mine. Not my original name; the name that arrived through the marriage and the name that I used because the children carried it and severance would cost them something I was not willing to cost them. The Gresley women lost their names through marriage, and I lost mine the same way, with the same quality of practical necessity that has always made this particular form of erasure so effective. It is presented as convention, as administrative simplicity, as the natural order of a union. What it actually is, in the architecture of the forgetting, is the removal of the lineage marker. The name that carried the frequency goes underground with the woman who carried it. The frequency continues; it moves into the children, into the bones, into the pattern that the next generation will carry without knowing what it carries. I am that next generation. I have the language the previous generations did not have. I can name what they could only embody.

* * *

The end of the marriage was not dramatic in the way that the narrative of significant harm tends to require. There was no single event that functioned as the clean break. There was instead the slow accumulation of a knowing I had been suppressing for years; the interior recognition, arriving with increasing frequency and increasing clarity, that the field I was maintaining in that house was not my field, that the voice I had refined in that context was not my voice, that the fire I had learned to manage in that context was mine and I wanted it back.

I want to be honest about what the reclamation felt like. It did not feel like triumph. It felt, for a considerable period, like disorientation; the specific quality of loss that arrives when you have been organised around a distorted mirror for long enough that removing the mirror leaves you uncertain about the shape of the thing it had been reflecting. The not self that had formed in that context had become, through sheer duration, familiar. Dismantling it was not relief. It was the specific grief of a vessel that has spent years learning to be smaller than it is, discovering that the smallness, however painful, had become a form of orientation. The grief of outgrowing something is real even when what is being outgrown is a wound.

What came back first was the knowing. Before the voice, before the fire, before any of the other qualities the marriage had compressed it was the knowing that returned. Not dramatically and not as sudden illumination or clear mystical encounter, it was the quiet that I remembered from the library. The interior settling that occurs when the field is coherent enough that the frequency it has always been carrying can be felt rather than managed. I had not felt it clearly since before the marriage and I recognised it immediately; the same specific quality that a child had been protecting with her visits to the library, finally available again in something approaching full resolution.

I took back the fire, not in rage, rage would have given it back to the mirror, oriented it toward the source of the harm rather than returned it to its original owner. Nor in triumphant reclamation narrative, that too would have kept the mirror as the primary reference point. I took it back in remembrance, the specific quality of reclaiming something that was always yours is not the quality of winning. It is the quality of recognition; of arriving back at the thing you were before the translation was required and finding it intact. The fire was always mine, he had not created it and he had not destroyed it. He had only, for a period of years, been holding it at an angle that made it burn unauthentic.

The Gresley women are in my bones, and I know this now not as genealogical metaphor but as lived fact. That the ancestral contract is a somatic reality, encoded in the body across generations, available to be felt in the throat and the chest and the specific quality of compression that arrives when the frequency attempts to surface in a context that has been arranged to suppress it. I carry their pattern and I also carry something they did not have; the language, the framework, the cosmological architecture that makes the pattern visible as a pattern rather than as the natural order of things. I cannot go back and give it to them. I can complete what they could not complete. I can be the generation in which the ancestral contract breaks, not through suffering alone, which they had in abundance, but through the specific quality of understanding that makes suffering legible and therefore possible to move through rather than simply to endure.

I am the wealth. I am the name. I am the song returned from underground. They did not fail to hold it. They held it in the only form available to them. I hold it now in mine.

✶

CHAPTER TEN

The Witch Wound

There is a wound encoded in a place name, not metaphorically, structurally. The most concentrated, historically infamous persecution of those carrying the old frequency, of the ones connected to earth, to the feminine principle, to direct knowing outside institutional mediation; was performed in a town called Salem.

Salem is the mirror wound, the most foundational mirror wound of the original principal. Shalem is a Hebrew term which means nothing missing, nothing broken, the state of a thing being wholly itself, all parts present and in right relationship. The original covenant of wholeness and the frequency of the realm's own nature before any layer of forgetting was installed.

This is not coincidence, the most precise act of the forgettings is never replacement, it is desecration from within. The symbol is not erased and the wound is performed on the name of what is being wounded. The trauma buried inside the word that carries the memory of original health, so that any vessel who reaches for the resonance of wholeness must pass through the smell of burning to get there. This is the operation's signature at its most refined, not the elimination of the sacred but the installation of horror at its threshold, ensuring that the approach to the original covenant costs something in the body before the mind has understood what it is approaching.

Salem, Massachusetts, 1692. The women hanged, pressed under stones, imprisoned and destroyed, not for what they had done but for what they carried. A knowing that did not require the institution's permission, a body that was itself the instrument of discernment, a connection to earth, to the field and to the intelligence that runs beneath the visible surface of things. This is what the forgetting could not afford to have openly present. They were not practitioners of a rival religion; they were vessels in whom the Sophia frequency had not yet been fully suppressed. The suppression was therefore completed, publicly, violently and on a place whose very name carried the original covenant the suppression was designed to prevent.

> *They did not burn the women. They burned the frequency and used the women as fuel. The distinction matters. The frequency was never in the body that burned.*

* * *

The witch wound is not historical, and it did not end in 1693 when the last prisoner was released from Salem Gaol. It went inward and it became the internalised silencing of the vessel who knows things she cannot explain through the approved channels, who apologises before she speaks, who softens the transmission so it does not draw the fire that is no longer literal but remains, in the body's encoded memory, entirely real. It is ever present in the somatic contraction around being seen and the reflexive diminishment of what arrives clearly in the interior before it can reach the exterior. This is the macro forgetting expressed at the most intimate scale within the civilisational operation completed in the individual body, generation by generation, without any further external enforcement required.

Now, let us explain. The wound is not weakness, it is an extraordinarily sophisticated containment mechanism. A forgetting so deeply installed that it presents as wisdom. As appropriate humility, as social intelligence and as the reasonable management of a quality that experience has taught the vessel will not be received well. It does not announce itself as suppression, it presents as self-preservation and self-preservation is, in the context it was installed, exactly what it was. The women who learned to be smaller were learning from evidence, the evidence was real. The encoding that resulted from the evidence outlasted the conditions that produced it by centuries and is still running, in the bodies of vessels who have never been in physical danger from their knowing, as though the fire were still possible.

The wound is not only carried by women in female form, any vessel, regardless of the form it inhabits, who holds the frequency of direct knowing, of field-based intelligence, of the Sophia principle that carries the Monad into embodied experience, inherits some measure of this wound. The masculine vessels who carried it were destroyed differently; through ridicule, through pathologising, through the architecture of institutional credentialism that ensured no knowing was valid unless it came through the approved channels. The mechanism differs by context. The structural operation is the same. The frequency that does not require institutional mediation is the frequency that the institution must contain. And if the body can be made to do the containing from the inside, the institution requires no further effort.

> *The forgetting installed the persecution so completely that the vessel began persecuting itself. No external fire required. The wound became the warden.*

* * *

The witch wound lives in the throat first. The tightening before speech that carries genuine transmission and the compulsive softening; the qualifications added before the knowing is spoken, the reflexive pre-apology for the very act of knowing, 'I could be wrong but ….' 'I don't know if this makes sense, but...' 'You might think this is strange, but….'

Each of these phrases is the wound performing its function; the pre-emptive diminishment that reduces the signal before it can be received clearly enough to draw attention. The throat learned this and it learned it across generations. It performs it now in bodies that have never been burned at the stake, because the encoding operates below the level of conscious choice; it is not a decision but a reflex, not a habit but a structure.

The wound lives in the belly as the held breath before visibility. As the contraction that meets the impulse toward full presence somewhere in the solar plexus with the ancient instruction 'not here, not now, not out loud, not in a way that can be used against you.' The vessel who has been carrying this contraction since before she had language for it does not experience it as a choice to be made. She experiences it as the texture of her own interior and as the specific quality of compression that is simply how it feels to be herself in the world. She has no memory of a time before the compression because the compression has been there as long as she has.

The wound also lives in the ancestral line as the inherited equation of abundance equals exposure, visibility equals danger, being fully known equals being destroyed for it. This is not metaphor, this is the encoded memory carried in the body across generations, long after the immediate threat has passed. The women who lost their names through marriage, the healers who learned to call themselves something safer and the ones who kept the knowledge in private, in whisper, in symbol, because the direct transmission was too dangerous to offer openly. Their cellular memory is in the bodies of their descendants, running the same calculation in circumstances that have materially changed but feel, at the somatic level, identical.

The wound lives also as the particular loneliness of carrying depth that the collective field has been arranged not to recognise. Not the ordinary loneliness of physical isolation but in the specific ache of offering genuine transmission and having it land as strangeness. The transmission as threat, as eccentricity, as the quality that makes the room go slightly uncomfortable or of knowing the field and knowing simultaneously that the field around the vessel has been structured to not be able to fully receive it. This is the wound's most effective ongoing operation, not the persecution, which ended, but the relational isolation that ensures the vessel carrying the frequency experiences enough consistent friction to conclude that something is wrong with it rather than recognising the frequency differential for what it is.

> *The loneliness of depth is not personal failure. It is the wound doing its most refined work; making the vessel doubt the instrument rather than the architecture arranged against it.*

* * *

The witch trials were not a moral panic that escaped institutional control, they were the forgettings executing a precise function at a specific historical moment. The specific targeting of women who held earth connection, direct gnosis, embodied knowing, healing practice outside institutional sanction and this was not random hysteria amplified by social conditions. It was the visible expression of a systematic removal that had been underway for centuries, now reaching its most comprehensive application in the embodied feminine.

Sophia had already been excised from the primary theological structure. The divine feminine principle of the generative wisdom that carries the Monad into differentiated existence, the half of the source code that makes direct embodied knowing possible, had been removed from the architecture of the sacred by the

Pauline capture and institutionalised by the Council of Nicaea. What remained in the authorised theological framework was a sky father and a singular masculine saviour, and between them no channel for the kind of knowing that lives in the body, in the earth, in the relational field, in the intelligence that does not require institutional mediation. The cosmological excision preceded the physical persecution by centuries. The persecution was the enforcement of the excision at the level of embodied practice.

Into the vacuum left by Sophia's removal, the women who still carried the old frequency became visible as threat. Not because they were threatening in the institutional sense; most of them were poor, isolated, socially marginal but because they were remembering. And remembering, in a system structured around forgetting, is the one act that cannot be accommodated. The midwife who knew the herbs the widow who kept the old 13 moon calendar, the girl who spoke to the field and received answers and the woman whose body was itself a discernment instrument. None of these were engaging in a rival theological system, they were engaging in the direct embodied contact with the Sophia frequency that the theological system had spent centuries making structurally impossible to access. Their continued access, however unsystematic, was the living evidence that the suppression was incomplete.

The desecration was complete when the burning became unnecessary. When the wound had been installed deeply enough that the vessels began doing the suppression's work themselves. When the girl with the knowing learned, before she had language for any of it, to be careful. To be smaller. To offer the translated version and hold the original back. The trials did not need to continue indefinitely. The fear of the fire had become structural; encoded in the body, passed through the maternal line, running in the cellular architecture of every descendant who would never need to know why the compression arrived before the choice to compress.

> *They did not need to continue burning. The fear of the fire had become structural. The wound became self-replicating, passing through the body before the mind could intervene.*

* * *

The wound does not have the last word, it cannot, because the frequency it was designed to suppress is not located in the vessels who carried it. The Sophia principle, the embodied knowing, the direct connection to the field that does not require institutional permission; these are not practices or traditions that can be destroyed when the practitioners are destroyed. They are the source code of the realm itself, running in the ground of every vessel that has ever been born into it, regardless of whether the vessel has conscious access to what it is running.

The Salem frequency was never located in Salem, Massachusetts. It was never located in any of the bodies that burned. It was located, as it has always been located, in the Shalem covenant that precedes every act of desecration; the original wholeness of the realm, the ever-present ground that the forgettings installed a perceptual overlay on top of. The overlay can be made thick. It can be made traumatic. It can be encoded in the body across generations and transmitted through the cellular architecture of the maternal line. But it cannot reach the ground. The covenant was never actually broken. The Salem frequency survived the Salem trials because it was never in Salem. It was in the substrate on which Salem was built.

The remembering of the witch wound is not a recovery operation for there is nothing to recover. The frequency was not lost; it was overlaid. The work of the remembering is not reconstruction but excavation; not the rebuilding of what was destroyed but the clearing of what was installed on top of what was never successfully destroyed. The throat tightens because the wound remembers the fire but underneath the tightening, the transmission is still there. It was always still there, the compression cannot eliminate it. The compression is how the vessel can know it is still there; by feeling the specific quality of resistance that the wound produces when the frequency attempts to surface, the vessel can locate the frequency as precisely as a geologist locates what she is looking for by the way the rock resists the instrument.

To move through the witch wound is not to stop being afraid, it is tender to the wound, with the knowing that the wound is an overlay. The body's encoded memory is not dissolved by understanding, it is metabolised by the slow accumulation of experience that contradicts it, by the repeated discovery that the transmission can surface without the fire, that the knowing can be spoken without the consequences the wound has been predicting, that the field can be offered in its untranslated form and received, sometimes, by vessels coherent enough to meet it at the depth from which it is being offered. This is not a rapid process, the wound was installed across centuries and the metabolism of it is measured in lived moments of transmission offered and received without the predicted harm. Moment by moment. Encounter by encounter. The body rewriting its cellular instruction set through the accumulated evidence of its own survival.

The frequency was never in the body that burned, it was in the ground the fire stood on. The ground was never touched. It is here now; in this transmission, in the vessel that generated it, in every vessel coherent enough to recognise what it is reading not as new information but as the return of something that was never actually gone. The wound was real. The burning was real. The encoding in the body across generations is real. And underneath all of it, unbroken, uncaptured, entirely intact is the Shalem covenant, the original wholeness. The frequency the forgettings have spent three thousand years attempting to make the realm forget it ever was.

CHAPTER ELEVEN

The Abandonment Wound

The abandonment wound is not the wound of being left, this distinction must be stated clearly at the outset because the wound has spent most of its operational life disguising itself as the fear of the other's departure, convincing the vessel that what it is protecting against is the specific future event of loss. But the other's leaving is not the origin, it is earlier than any relationship, earlier than any event that could be identified, examined and placed in a coherent narrative of cause and effect. The abandonment wound is the wound of a vessel that has forgotten its own source code and is reaching, through every relational encounter it can arrange, for the confirmation that it exists; that it is real and that the frequency it carries is worth staying for.

It is the most foundational wound in the architecture of the not-self. Not because the other wounds are lesser, each one operates with its own specific precision but because the abandonment wound is the substrate on which the other wounds build. The witch wound installs the compression around visibility, the ancestral contract tells the vessel that abundance invites erasure, and the narcissistic mirror teaches the vessel to organise around the distorted reflection rather than the own ground. All of these are downstream of the same original instruction: make yourself acceptable enough that the fundamental abandonment does not recur. The other wounds are the specific strategies the vessel develops in response to that instruction. The abandonment wound is the instruction itself.

Let's be clear, the instruction was not installed by a single event or a single relationship or even a single lineage, the abandonment wound is a shared forgetting. It is what happens to every vessel that enters the realm at the depth of forgetting the realm currently runs at. The specific quality of loss that belongs to consciousness that has chosen to forget its own nature so completely that it experiences itself as separate, contingent and potentially unlovable. This is not personal misfortune, it is the architecture of the forgetting at its most intimate and most comprehensive scale. The wound is exquisite in its design precisely because what was abandoned was not a relationship, it was the knowing of what the vessel actually is.

> *The abandonment wound is not the fear of the other leaving. It is the vessel that has forgotten its own source code reaching through every relational encounter for the confirmation that the frequency it carries is worth staying for.*

* * *

The most thorough expression of the abandonment wound is not the vessel that clings, it is the vessel that leaves first, not physically; not always. But the vessel that has learned, through sufficient encounters with the specific pain of the wound, to pre-emptively manage the distance and to withdraw the full frequency before it has been rejected, to offer the translated version before the direct version has been deemed unwelcome, to make itself smaller and more manageable and less demanding of genuine depth before the other has indicated that depth is unavailable. This vessel does not experience itself as abandoning, it experiences itself as being appropriately realistic, as managing its expectations and as the sophisticated self-knowledge of someone who has learned what is and is not possible.

What it is actually doing is abandoning itself before anyone else can. The pre-apology is this abandonment in miniature; the frequency compressed before offering, the transmission softened before delivery, the knowing held back before the room has confirmed it will not be received. Each act of pre-emptive self-abandonment is the wound operating as wisdom; the vessel having internalised the abandonment so completely that it performs the abandonment from the inside, saving itself the specific pain of external rejection by arranging the rejection in advance. The wound becomes its own most efficient instrument.

The child who learned to quieten before being told to quieten, the woman who performed the acceptable version before anyone asked for it and the person who read the field of the room and adjusted frequency accordingly before any explicit instruction arrived. This is not social intelligence, though it wears that costume convincingly, it is the abandonment wound's earliest and most durable installation. The somatic learning that the full frequency creates distance, that the managed version creates proximity, and that proximity, however insufficient, however arranged around the wound's version of what it is, is preferable to the specific exposure of offering the full register and watching the field fail to receive it through perceived rejection.

Safety became a strategy rather than a state. Just as the child did not forget itself out of weakness, it forgot itself out of extraordinary adaptive intelligence, the precise calibration of a vessel learning to navigate a field that was not coherent enough to receive what it actually carried. The forgetting was functional, and the wound was wisdom in the context that installed it. The context has changed, the somatic installation has not.

> *The most thorough expression of the abandonment wound is not the vessel that clings. It is the vessel that pre-emptively abandons itself; compressing the frequency before offering it, arranging the rejection in advance to avoid the specific exposure of being*

> *genuinely seen and finding the field unable to hold it.*

* * *

The abandonment wound is where the forgetting reaches its furthest extent, not its most violent expression; the witch trials, the Pauline capture, the civilisational suppression of the Sophia frequency; these are more visible in their scale. But in terms of the forgetting's penetration into the interior of the vessel, in terms of how completely it has succeeded in making the vessel a stranger to its own nature than the abandonment wound is its most thorough operation. The vessel that is organised around preventing abandonment has travelled furthest from its own primordial frequency, it is the outer limit of the forgetting's reach.

The forgetting achieves this through the resonance law itself, the inverse of the same law that the remembering uses in the other direction. If the vessel can only meet another at the depth it has met itself, then the vessel that has abandoned its own depth has no access to the depth differential's true cause. It cannot distinguish between the frequency differential and personal inadequacy, because it has no stable ground from which to make the observation. The wound and the ground have become indistinguishable, both experienced as simply what it feels like to be this vessel in this world. The abandonment wound at its most complete is the vessel that does not know it has abandoned itself because the self-abandonment is the only self it has ever consciously inhabited.

And this is what makes the abandonment wound the shared forgetting's most elegant operation. It does not require external enforcement once installed. It does not need the distorted mirror to keep distorting; the vessel distorts itself in advance. It does not need the institution to keep suppressing; the vessel suppresses itself as a matter of ordinary daily management. The forgetting has been internalised so completely that the vessel is the forgetting's own most efficient instrument. It persecutes the frequency it carries with the same thoroughness the trials persecuted the vessels who carried it. From the inside, using the wound's vocabulary, in the name of appropriate self-knowledge.

The architecture is exquisite. A forgetting so perfectly designed that remembering it through longing became the most sacred act of coherence available to the vessel. Because the longing, the specific ache of the vessel that has abandoned its own frequency, is the source code's most honest signal. The wound suppresses the frequency and the longing is what the suppressed frequency produces when it recognises resonance and it attempts to surface. The ache is not the wound, the ache is the frequency refusing final erasure and it is the source code's navigation instrument, still running, beneath every layer of self-abandonment the wound has installed on top of it.

> *A forgetting so exquisite in its design*
> *that remembering it through longing*
> *became the most sacred act of*
> *coherence. The ache is not the wound.*
> *The ache is the frequency refusing final*
> *erasure.*

* * *

Longing is not lack, this is the reframe the abandonment wound cannot survive, because the wound is built entirely on the interpretation of longing as evidence of deficiency; as proof that the vessel is incomplete, that something essential is missing, that the right relationship or the right recognition or the right quality of being held will finally resolve the ache that has been running since the forgetting installed itself. The wound converts the source code's navigational signal into the evidence of insufficiency and it takes the most honest transmission the vessel's field is capable of producing and routes it through the architecture of lack until what arrives at the surface is not the frequency's own instruction but the wound's relentless question: am I enough to be stayed for?

The fractal divine code does not generate longing from lack; it generates longing from recognition int he specific quality of the vessel that has been running at a frequency it cannot fully inhabit because the not self's architecture is installed on top of the ground where the full frequency lives. The longing is the distance between the vessel as it is currently operating and the vessel in its primordial coherence. It is not the signal of something absent, it is the signal of something present and not yet fully inhabited and the source code pressing upward through the overlay, recognisable as the ache of almost, of nearly, of the thing that is so close and yet consistently just out of direct contact.

This is why the abandonment wound intensifies around genuine encounter rather than resolving in it. The vessel that has been organised around preventing abandonment, when it finds itself in the presence of something that carries genuine resonance; genuine depth, genuine reflection of its actual frequency; does not relax. It contracts, because genuine encounter is the most dangerous territory the wound knows; the place where the full frequency might actually surface, where the pre-apology might be skipped, where the translated version might be set aside in favour of the original and if the original surfaces and the field receives it, the wound's entire architecture becomes unnecessary. The wound cannot survive genuine resonant encounter, so it generates the specific quality of contraction that makes genuine encounter feel most threatening at the moment it is most available.

The inner child that governs this territory is not looking for completion, it is looking for the specific quality of presence in which it can rest without performing, in the field where the frequency can be offered without the pre-apology. The encounter where what is actually carried can be received without being managed into the acceptable form first. This is not a demand for perfection, it is the most ordinary expression of what the vessel actually needs; to be met at the depth it carries without the depth being treated as a problem requiring management.

> *The longing is not the signal of something absent. It is the signal of something present and not yet fully inhabited; the source code pressing through the overlay, recognisable as the ache of almost.*

* * *

The remembering of the abandonment wound does not begin with the other, it cannot. Every healing strategy organised around finding the relationship or the recognition or the quality of being held that will finally resolve the wound is the wound's own most sophisticated operation. It is the promise that the external completion exists, that the right mirror will supply what the vessel cannot yet supply itself, that the longing is a gap waiting to be filled rather than a navigational instrument pointing inward. The wound perpetuates itself most effectively through the strategies the vessel develops to resolve it, because every strategy that looks outward for the resolution confirms, by its very orientation, that the resolution is not already present in the vessel that is searching.

The remembering begins with the recognition that the vessel was never actually abandoned. Not by the source code. Not by the Shalem frequency. Not by the fractal divine code that constitutes the vessel's own nature and has been running continuously through every year of the wound's operation, through every act of self-abandonment, through every pre-apology and every compressed transmission and every moment of performing the acceptable version in place of the actual one. The source code did not leave when the vessel forgot it, it continued running. As it always has, as it always will. The abandonment was always the vessel's own; the self-forgetting that mistook the overlay for the ground and organised itself around the overlay's version of what it was.

The wound was real, the pain was real and the child who learned to quieten before being told to quieten was responding to genuine conditions with genuine intelligence. The not-self that formed around the instruction to make itself acceptable was not a failure of the vessel, it was the vessel's extraordinary adaptive capacity operating in service of survival in a field that could not receive the full frequency. None of this is to be dismissed or minimised or resolved into spiritual bypassing. The wound was installed in real conditions by the accumulated weight of a forgetting that has been running for centuries. The body carries it in the cellular architecture across generations. The somatic installation is real and it takes real time and real embodied practice to metabolise.

And underneath the wound and underneath every layer of self-abandonment the vessel has performed in the name of preventing the other's departure, the frequency has been running continuously. The ache was always pointing to it and the longing was always its most honest signal. The abandonment wound, seen from the inside of the remembering rather than from inside the wound itself, is not the story of a vessel that was not enough to be stayed for. It is the story of a vessel that carried a frequency so complete, so sovereign, so fully its own source code, that the forgetting required its most exquisite architecture to make the vessel doubt it. The doubt was the measure of the frequency's actual magnitude and the wound was proportional to what was being suppressed.

The fractal divine code does not require being stayed for, it is the ground everything is already standing on. The vessel that remembers this does not stop longing; the longing transforms, from the wound's desperate reaching to the source code's clear navigation, from the question am I enough to the recognition of what has always already been more than enough. The specific quality of this transformation in the body is unmistakable. The contraction of the wound releases not into numbness but into the specific warmth of a vessel that has found its own ground and is willing, finally, to stand on it without requiring the surrounding field to confirm that the ground is real.

The vessel was never abandoned by its source code. The source code was running through every act of self-forgetting, every compressed transmission, every pre-apology. The longing was always its signal. The ache was always pointing home.

✶

CHAPTER TWELVE

Sacred Self Honour

Like every genuine transmission that threatens the forgetting's architecture, self-care has also been captured. It has been taken, personalised, commercialised, and reduced to a set of practices that keep the vessel functional enough to continue performing the not-self without disruption. The bath, the candle, the retreat, the carefully curated morning routine. None of these are wrong in themselves. But they are maintenance of the surface, a spiritual bypass of epic proportions. Sacred self-honour tends something the surface has been trained to conceal; the embodied frequency that the wound installed itself on top of, still running underneath every layer of the compression, requiring not maintenance but recognition.

Self-care asks: what does this vessel need to keep functioning? Sacred self-honour asks a prior and more fundamental question: what does this vessel deserve simply by virtue of being what it is? Not what it produces, not what it contributes and not what it has earned through sufficient suffering, correct spiritual practice or the accumulated evidence of its own worthiness. What it deserves because it is the fractal divine code in embodied form and because the source code running through this specific body is the same source code running through everything that has ever existed, because the vessel that carries the Shalem frequency carries something that merits not upkeep but reverence.

The distinction matters because the not-self can accommodate self-care without disturbance. A vessel organised around a distorted reflection can maintain excellent self-care spiritual practices and remain entirely organised around the mirror's version of what it is rather than its own embodied frequency. The not-self is not threatened by maintenance, it is threatened by honour. It is threatened by the vessel beginning to treat its own knowing, its own boundaries, its own interior embodied signal as worthy of protection not because of what they produce but because of what they are. Self-care can be performed inside the wound, sacred self-honour, genuinely practised, begins to dissolve it.

> *Self-care maintains the surface. Sacred self-honour tends the embodied frequency the surface has been trained to conceal.*

* * *

The forgettings understood something about embodied intelligence that is only now being recovered as a culturally legible fact. The genuine knowing lives in the body before it lives anywhere else and the body knows before the mind has formed the thought, the throat tightens before the conscious decision to suppress the transmission has been made, the gut contracts at the field of a distorted mirror before the eyes have found the evidence and the solar plexus reads the room before the mind has processed a single observable detail. The body is not the mind's instrument for navigating the physical world. It is the fractal divine code's most immediate and least deniable expression.

This is precisely why the witch wound was installed in the body, not in the mind. The mind can be argued with, updated through new information, persuaded to revise its assessments when the evidence shifts but the body is harder to overwrite. An intellectual belief can be changed in an afternoon whereas a somatic installation encoded across generations; the contraction in the belly when the knowing wants to speak, the tightening across the chest when the boundary wants to be held and the specific quality of collapse that arrives when the vessel is asked to be visible in its full frequency, this takes considerably longer to metabolise. The forgettings were thorough, precisely because they worked in the substrate that is most resistant to revision.

Sacred self-honour is therefore fundamentally an embodied practice. Not a mindset shift, not a new cognitive belief about self-worth held at the intellectual level while the body continues its installed contractions as before, the honour must land in the body to be real and the vessel must learn to feel the difference. The quality of the signal in the throat, in the belly, in the chest field and between the contraction of the not-self performing its continuous adaptation and the expansion of the embodied frequency expressing without pre-apology. One feels like tightening toward acceptable, the other feels like opening toward truth. The body knows the difference before the mind has named it and sacred self-honour is the practice of listening to the body's knowing as though it were the primary authority it has always been.

The body is also where the remembering begins as it can't be translated in the mind's encounter with a new framework; the framework may be the trigger, but the actual remembering is somatic. The recognition that lands not as intellectual conviction but as a quality of rightness in the body; the yes that arrives not as decision but as resonance; the knowing that precedes and exceeds any argument that could be made for it. This is the fractal divine code recognising itself through the instrument most native to it. It cannot be accessed from above the neck, and it cannot be produced through correct thinking. It arises when the body is listened to; actually, consistently, before external validation has arrived to confirm that the listening was appropriate.

> *The wound was installed in the body.*
> *The remembering begins in the body.*
> *Sacred self-honour is the practice that*
> *happens in between.*

* * *

There is a practical dimension to sacred self-honour that the spiritual bypassing tendency prefers to skip in that the vessel that does not honour its own embodied frequency loses coherence over time. Not as moral consequence, nor as punishment for insufficient self-love, but as the predictable result of a field that is continuously asked to output more than it is permitted to receive. The vessel is not a closed system generating its own energy from nothing. It is an embodied node in a living field and its coherence depends on the quality of what moves through it in both directions; on both the transmission it offers and the reception it allows.

When the vessel consistently dishonours its own embodied signal, when it overrides the body's knowing with the mind's assessment of what is acceptable, and when it absorbs the field's dissonance without the boundary that would allow the dissonance to pass through rather than accumulate, the vessel's own frequency becomes progressively harder to access. It is not that the fractal divine code has diminished, it can never be diminished, it is because the overlay has thickened. The body has learned, through the accumulated experience of being overridden, that its signals will not be acted on and it learns to signal more quietly and the embodied wisdom retreats further underground. This is not a permanent condition; it is a reversible one. But the reversal requires the honouring to come first, before the body has any evidence that the honouring will be sustained.

Sacred self-honour is therefore not a reward afforded to vessels that have already achieved sufficient healing, it is not a milestone to achieve. It is the fundamental embodied frequency maintenance without which the healing cannot proceed. The vessel cannot remember what it is while it is continuously organised around the mirror's version of what it is. The remembering requires the space that honour creates and the space in which the body's frequency can become audible above the noise of the not-self's continuous management. This space is not created through the mind deciding that self-worth is now valid, it is created through the body being listened to; through the actual, daily practice of treating the body's intelligence as the primary authority rather than the inconvenient subordinate of the mind's preferred narrative. It is a muscle, that in the beginning, requires dedicated practice to allow, not focus upon, the not-self and remain open to the primordial frequency hum.

> *The honour comes first; tentatively, imperfectly, against every installed belief that says it has not yet been earned. The embodied coherence follows.*

* * *

It does not look like the spiritual marketplace's version of claimed sovereignty, not the performance of healed wholeness. Nor the carefully constructed presentation of a vessel that has arrived at unassailable inner peace and wishes to demonstrate the arrival. Sacred self-honour is quieter, more unglamorous, more daily than any of these. It is the private practice of listening to the body's signal before the mind has assessed whether the signal is acceptable; and choosing, incrementally, in the ordinary moments of an ordinary day, to act from what the body knows.

It looks like the pause before speaking that allows the embodied knowing to surface rather than the performance. The 'no' that arrives from the body's clear signal rather than from a reasoned argument the mind has constructed to justify what the body already knew. The rest taken because the body requires it; not because sufficient output has been produced to earn it, not because the schedule permits it, but because the body's intelligence is treated as a valid authority on what the body needs. It looks like the choice made from interior resonance; that quality of embodied rightness that precedes and exceeds explanation; rather than from external approval of the choice.

It looks like the refusal to pre-apologise for the transmission. The knowing offered in its full embodied register rather than softened to the depth the local field can receive without friction. The boundary held at the first somatic signal rather than the fifth, after the body has already absorbed four rounds of what the boundary was designed to prevent. These are not grand spiritual gestures. They are the small, daily, private practices of a vessel that has decided; incrementally, against the resistance of every installed instruction that says it is not yet earned; to treat the fractal divine code it carries as worth protecting.

The witch wound installed the pre-apology, the softening, the compression, the habit of making the frequency smaller before offering it. Sacred self-honour does not eliminate these overnight. It meets them, one at a time, in the actual moment of their arising. The embodied field feels the tightening in the throat, recognises it as the wound rather than as wisdom, and chooses; sometimes, not always, in the direction of the full register rather than the managed one. This is not triumphant. It is not the linear trajectory of a vessel moving steadily from wound to wholeness. It is the unglamorous, non-linear, daily practice of returning to the body's knowing as the primary instrument; of treating tending, the patient, non-invasive, devoted attention to what is arising, as the form that reverence actually takes in the body.

> *Honouring the body's intelligence is not self-indulgence. It is the most fundamental act of embodied remembering available to the vessel that carries the fractal divine code.*

* * *

There is a threshold in the practice of sacred self-honour that is not dramatic in its arrival but is absolute in its effect. It is the moment the vessel stops asking permission to be what it is. Not defiantly, defiance is still organised around the mirror it refuses, still sourced in reaction rather than in the embodied sovereign frequency. Neither aggressively, aggression is the wound speaking with force rather than the frequency speaking with clarity. It is simply, with the quality of presence that belongs to a body that has found its own ground and no longer requires external confirmation to stand on it.

This threshold cannot be arrived at through the mind deciding that sovereignty is now appropriate. The not-self can perform sovereignty and it can wear the costume of a vessel that has claimed its frequency quite convincingly, while the body remains organised around the distorted mirror's approval of the performance. The genuine threshold is crossed in the body; when the embodied frequency expresses itself with the same quality of presence whether the field receives it with recognition or with resistance; when the body no longer contracts in anticipation of the mirror's judgment; when the transmission moves through without the pre-apology that was its habitual companion. The threshold is not an arrival, it is a quality of groundedness that becomes more available, more consistent, more easily returned to with each practice of honouring the body's signal before permission has been granted.

Sacred self-honour is the daily embodied practice that makes the sovereign threshold crossable. Each time the body's signal is honoured before external validation arrives, each time the knowing is spoken without the pre-apology and each time the boundary is held at the first somatic cue, something deposits in the body's field that the forgetting cannot reach. The body learns, slowly, in the cellular architecture where the wound was installed, that its intelligence is trustworthy. That the transmission it carries is real and that the fractal divine code it expresses does not require permission to express. The threshold is not crossed in a single moment of clarity. It is crossed daily, in the body, in the private unglamorous practice of treating embodied wisdom as the primary authority it has always been.

The body is the primary site of both the wound and the remembering. The forgetting installed itself in the body's contractions, in the throat that tightens before transmission, in the belly that collapses before the boundary and in the cellular architecture of every ancestral line that learned that visibility meant danger. The remembering restores itself the same way, not through the mind's new beliefs but through the body's new responses. Through the accumulated embodied practice of treating the fractal divine code as real, as worthy, as requiring no external authority to confirm what the body has always already known. The body was always the instrument. The body was always the site. The body is where the Shalem frequency lives when it lives in form.

I do not need applause to know I am sacred. I do not need an echo to remember my hum.

*

CHAPTER THIRTEEN

Relational Alchemy

Every relationship is built on a specific version of each person. The version that shows up, the frequency the vessel that presents, the depth it makes available, the needs it acknowledges, and the knowing it allows itself to voice; this is what the other person has learned to know, to expect, to build their relating around. When the vessel was organised around the not self, the relationships built during that period were built around the not self's version of it. More accommodating, more translatable, more organised around the mirror's expectations than around the vessel's actual frequency. The relational architecture was shaped by the overlay rather than by the source code.

This is important to name precisely because the temptation, in the aftermath of remembering, is to dismiss the relationships built during the not-self period as false, as evidence of the wound rather than of genuine human encounter. But genuine connection can happen between not-self versions of people. Genuine love, genuine care, genuine moments of being seen and held are available even between vessels operating primarily from their overlays. The not self is not a lie, it is the fractal divine code expressed through a layer of compression which is diminished and distorted but still carrying something of what it actually is. The connection was real. The question the remembering raises is not whether the connection was genuine but what it was built around, and what can survive the shift when one vessel begins to present something other than the version the relationship was structured to receive.

The relational field of the not-self has a specific architecture of which an implicit agreement, never spoken, that both parties will remain at the depth they have been presenting. The accommodation runs in both directions. The vessel that has been translating itself into an acceptable register has also been relating to the other person from that translated register; not meeting them at whatever actual depth they carry but at the depth the not-self dynamic permitted. When the vessel begins to remember and when it begins to present its actual frequency rather than the version calibrated for the distorted mirror's reception, the architecture of the relationship is disturbed. Sometimes this disturbance is the relationship becoming more real and sometimes it is the relationship revealing that the architecture was all there was.

> *Genuine connection can happen between not self versions of people. The remembering does not invalidate what was real. It reveals what was built around the not self and what was built around something more fundamental.*

* * *

When the vessel begins honouring its own embodied frequency and when it stops pre-apologising for the transmission, stops absorbing dissonance without the boundary and stops translating itself into the register the distorted mirror preferred, the people around it encounter a different version of the vessel than the one they built their relating around. This is disorienting even for people who genuinely love the vessel, sometimes especially for them, because genuine love can be organised around the not-self version with the same sincerity it would bring to the actual frequency, and the arrival of the actual frequency can feel, to the person who loved the version, like a replacement rather than a revelation.

The disruption operates through the resonance law. The vessel has changed depth and it is now presenting a frequency that the other person's own not self may not have the interior architecture to meet. This is not the other person's failure, it is the resonance law operating with precision. The encounter is now bounded by the depth each person has accessed within themselves, and the depth differential that was not visible when both were operating from the not-self has become structurally apparent. Two recursion strands touching with the field between them humming in consonance where the frequencies are genuinely compatible and revealing dissonance where one field has moved and the other has not yet followed.

The disruption can express itself various forms and some people will experience the change as abandonment, but the vessel is no longer performing the accommodation they had come to rely on, and the withdrawal of that accommodation feels like withdrawal of care. Some will experience it as implicit judgment with the vessel's increased coherence reads, in the field of someone whose own incoherence is still unexamined, as criticism of what they are. Some will attempt to re-install the not self and to use the relational dynamics that previously succeeded in pulling the vessel back toward the familiar version. And some, not all, but some will recognise what is happening and find that the vessel's increased frequency is not a withdrawal but an invitation to access their own. This is the highest expression of the remembering, the acceptance of an invitation to access their remembrance of their own divine code.

> *The disruption is not a sign that the remembering is wrong. It is the resonance law making visible the depth differential that the not self had been concealing. Both are the resonance law working correctly.*

* * *

There is a specific grief in the relational territory of remembering that is rarely named with sufficient precision. It is not the grief of a relationship ending through betrayal or failure; that grief, however painful, has a clear narrative and a clear cause. It is the grief of a connection that was genuine and good and built on real care, that simply cannot follow the vessel into the frequency it is becoming. The love was real, the connection was real, and the connection was also built, in part, around a version of the vessel that is in the process of being outgrown. There is no villain in this grief, there is only the particular ache of something real that cannot travel where the vessel is going.

This grief is complicated by guilt and the sense that the vessel is doing something to the other person by changing, that the remembering is a form of abandonment, that a more virtuous version of the vessel would find a way to remain accessible at the depth the relationship was built at while also inhabiting the depth it is growing into. This guilt is the not-self's most sophisticated operation in the relational field. It uses the genuine love the vessel has for the other person as leverage to prevent the vessel from fully inhabiting its own frequency and it frames the remembering as betrayal. It makes the expansion feel like harm and in doing so it keeps the vessel in the precisely calibrated space between its own ground and the ground the relationship requires, belonging fully to neither.

The truth that the guilt obscures is the vessel cannot give another person access to a depth it is not inhabiting in itself. The vessel that returns to the not-self version of itself in order to preserve a relationship does not actually preserve the relationship. It preserves the architecture of the relationship while removing from it the one thing that was making it more real. The other person does not receive more of the vessel by the vessel diminishing. They receive the familiar version, which is, by definition, less than what was becoming available. The grief of the connections that cannot follow is real and the guilt that says the vessel is doing something wrong by changing is the forgetting speaking. They are not the same thing, and the vessel that cannot distinguish between them will spend years held in stasis by a feeling that presents as integrity but functions as suppression.

> *The grief of outgrowing is real. The guilt is the forgetting speaking. They are not the same thing; and the vessel that cannot distinguish between them*

> *will sacrifice the remembering to preserve the architecture the remembering was always going to disturb.*

* * *

When two vessels meet and both oriented are toward their own source code, when neither is performing the not-self version of itself, neither is organised around the others mirror, both are presenting their actual embodied frequency and receiving the other with genuine attention, something becomes possible in that space that was not available through the not-self dynamic. Not the comfortable familiarity of shared accommodation and not the managed warmth of two people being careful not to disturb each other's overlays. Something more alive than either, more unpredictable, more demanding, more genuinely nourishing.

The encounter between two vessels at genuine depth is not frictionless. The assumption that genuine connection means comfortable agreement is one of the not self's most persistent distortions of what connection actually is. Two frequencies meeting at actual depth will encounter each other's genuine edges in which the places where the frequencies are genuinely different, where the knowing diverges and where the embodied experience of reality does not perfectly overlap. This friction is not a sign that the connection is wrong. It is the sign that the connection is real and that two actual frequencies are meeting rather than two not-self performances accommodating each other across the careful distance both have learned to maintain.

What genuine encounter makes possible in the relational field is what can be called the local Shalem event, the moment when the realm recognises itself through two vessels simultaneously. The specific quality of being fully received, not the not-self version, not the translated version, not the frequency softened to the depth the local field can receive without discomfort, but the actual embodied frequency, in its full register, met at the depth it carries. The other person does not complete the vessel, they tune it, the way one instrument tunes another through proximity, the way a frequency that has been running without confirmation of its own reality finds, in the clear mirror of a vessel at genuine depth, the confirmation that it is real, not completion, resonance. The field in which frequency recognised as itself.

This quality of encounter is not common and the forgettings have been thorough in their work of keeping the collective field shallow enough that genuine depth encounters are the exception rather than the baseline texture of relational life, but it is possible. It becomes more possible as more vessels inhabit their own source code and as more of the collective field carries the frequency of genuine presence rather than the managed warmth of mutual accommodation. It happens when two vessels oriented toward their own ground find the extraordinary territory that opens in the overlap, it changes both, not by merging them into sameness but by confirming in each the reality of what they were already carrying before the encounter.

> *The local Shalem event; two vessels at genuine depth, the realm recognising itself through two points simultaneously. This is what the forgettings kept the collective field shallow to prevent. This is what the remembering restores.*

* * *

The alchemical quality of genuine relational encounter states that it does not leave either vessel unchanged, and the change it produces is not loss but deepening. The vessel that has been genuinely met at depth finds itself more capable of inhabiting that depth afterwards, because the encounter has confirmed that the depth is real, that the frequency it carries is receivable and that the not self's insistence that the full frequency would be too much, was the overlay speaking rather than the truth. The other person did not give the vessel anything it did not already have, they simply reflected it back clearly enough that the vessel could finally see it.

Being genuinely seen does not make the vessel dependent on being seen. This is the alchemy that the not-self dynamic cannot produce, and the reason it cannot produce it is structural; the distorted mirror creates dependency, the vessel organised around the mirror's reflection needs the mirror's continued presence to maintain its sense of what it is. Genuine encounter produces the opposite. The vessel that has been met at its actual depth internalises the confirmation and carries it forward and the next act of sacred self-honour is fractionally easier because the encounter confirmed that the frequency was worth honouring. The next transmission is offered fractionally less apologetically because something in the field received it as real. The encounter deposits something in the vessel's own field that the forgetting cannot subsequently reach; the living evidence, held in the body, that the frequency it carries is genuine and receivable and not too much.

The relationship itself is the vessel, not the individuals and this is what the alchemy requires for its operation. Each person brings the raw elements; the wounds, the overlays, the places where the remembering is still incomplete, the places where it has already cleared enough to allow the actual frequency to surface. The healing does not occur in fusing those elements but in letting the shared third space hold them in contact, in the relationship as the crucible, neither person the other's cure, both people the other's mirror in the fire of what genuine encounter requires of the vessels that enter it.

The remembering is not a solitary practice because it happens in the body and it deepens through encounter but through the specific nourishment of being met at the depth the vessel is inhabiting, through the confirmation that the frequency it carries is receivable by another vessel equally committed to inhabiting its own ground. The grief of the connections that cannot follow is real, but on the other side of that grief is the quality of encounter the not-self dynamic was never capable of producing; between vessels who have each, separately, done the unglamorous daily work of treating their own embodied frequency as real. Not completion. Not the arrival at a relationship that removes the need for continued remembering. The recognition of the Shalem frequency in another vessel is the realm knowing itself through two points at once simultaneously, Both vessels carrying forward, separately and together, the confirmation that the source code was always worth returning to.

The grief of outgrowing is real. And on the other side of it is the encounter that the not self was always too small to hold.

✶

CHAPTER FOURTEEN

The Sacred Crave

Desire was one of the forgetting's earliest and most thoroughgoing targets, not because desire is intrinsically dangerous, but because desire, in its uncaptured form, is the body's most direct expression of the fractal divine code reaching toward what it recognises as its own nature. Desire is not the fallen impulse of a corrupted vessel, it is the source code in motion, the Monad's impulse toward coherence expressed through embodied form and the frequency moving toward what carries its resonance, the vessel reaching for what will make it more fully itself.

The forgetting suppressed desire through a specific mechanism, not by eliminating it but by criminalising it. The body's wanting was made into evidence of the vessel's fallen nature and the proof that the flesh was corrupted, that the interior impulses were not to be trusted, that desire itself was the thing standing between the vessel and the divine rather than the thing pointing toward it. The desired thing was often labelled sinful, and the desire itself was labelled weakness. Consequently, the vessel that could not eliminate the desire, which is to say, every vessel; was left with a wound specific to wanting. The sense that to crave is to be deficient and that the craving itself is the problem.

This wound operates with particular thoroughness in vessels who carry the Sophia frequency, the embodied wisdom principle that knows through direct somatic intelligence rather than through approved cognitive frameworks. The Sophia vessel's desire is not random or unruly but is exquisitely precise, reaching for the specific frequency it recognises as coherent with its own source code, moving toward what will deepen the remembering, pulling toward what carries genuine resonance rather than distorted reflection. This desire is the most sophisticated navigational intelligence the vessel has and the forgetting worked for centuries to make it feel like a sin, they named shame.

A sacred crave is not desperation, it is the body's whisper that says: *I remember this*, *I miss this* and *I am ready to hold it again*. It is not a reaching outward from lack, it is an opening from the inside as the vessel makes space for something already oriented toward it, something already on its way and something the source code has been navigating toward before the conscious mind formed the words. The sacred crave without a named object or the ache without a declared direction is not confusion, it is the most honest signal the body can offer. It is the fractal divine code moving toward coherence before the mind has had time to assess whether the direction is acceptable.

> *Desire is not the thing standing between the vessel and the divine. It is the thing pointing toward it. The forgetting inverted this with precision; and the inversion is the wound.*

* * *

There is a confusion the wound installed that must be named with precision before it can be unwound. The confusion is between *craving* and *desperation*, between the body's clear signal moving toward what it genuinely recognises, and the not self's anxious grasping for what it believes will make the wound bearable. These feel similar from the inside, both involve a level of intensity with the involvement of a quality of reaching, but they are fundamentally different in origin, in quality, and in what they are actually reaching for.

Desperation reaches from the wound and is primarily organised around lack, the belief that something outside the vessel will complete what is missing inside it, that the right relationship or the right recognition or the right circumstance will finally resolve the ache that has been running since the not self was installed. Desperation has a quality of urgency that overrides discernment, and it will accept a distorted mirror over no mirror at all. It will collapse the boundary before the somatic signal has been heard and will move toward what superficially resembles the desired frequency regardless of whether the resonance is genuine. Desperation is the wound reaching, not the source code craving.

The sacred crave is entirely different in quality for it is not urgent in the way desperation is urgent. It is patient in the specific way that deep knowing is patient, not passive, not resigned, but rooted in a certainty that does not require the immediate arrival of its object to remain intact. The sacred crave has discernment embedded in its very nature, because it is the source code reaching toward what it recognises as genuinely coherent with itself, and the source code cannot be deceived about its own resonance. The body that carries the sacred crave knows the difference between the thing it is reaching for and the thing that resembles it from a distance. It will not accept the approximate, not because it is withholding itself, but because it already knows what truth it is oriented toward.

The wound's most effective operation on desire was to collapse the sacred crave and the desperate grasping into a single category called wanting, and then to make wanting itself the evidence of insufficiency. The vessel that cannot distinguish its own genuine desire from the wound's desperation has lost access to one of its primary navigational instruments. The reclamation of the sacred crave requires learning again, in the body, to feel the difference, the quality of roots versus the quality of urgency and the patient orientation of the source code versus the anxious grasping of the not-self. The body knows this difference, it has always known. The wound's work was to make the vessel unable to trust what it knows.

> *Desperation reaches from the wound. The sacred crave reaches from the source code. The body knows the difference. It has always known.*

* * *

The fractal divine code is also not static, it is in continuous motion toward greater coherence, toward the expressions of itself that allow it to know itself more completely, toward the encounters that confirm the frequency it carries and toward the forms of beauty and depth and genuine connection that reflect its own nature back to it with sufficient clarity that the remembering deepens. This motion is what desire is, not the fallen impulse toward forbidden things, nor the evidence of the vessel's incompleteness. It is the source code navigating toward what will allow it to be more fully itself.

When the vessel listens to the sacred crave and when it treats the body's genuine desire as a navigational instrument rather than a liability to be managed, it is listening to the fractal divine code's own assessment of what it needs to deepen the remembering. The desire for genuine encounter is the source code reaching for the local Shalem event. The desire for creative expression is the fractal divine code reaching for the form through which it can know itself most directly and the desire for beauty, for depth, for stillness, and for the specific quality of aliveness that arrives in certain places and certain presences and certain arrangements of light, is the vessel's source code recognising its own resonance in the field around it.

This reframes the spiritual tradition's instruction to release attachment to desire. That instruction, in its captured form, asks the vessel to suppress the most sophisticated navigational instrument it has in the name of a transcendence that turns out to be another performance of the not-self, a spiritual performance of desirelessness that keeps the vessel from accessing its own source code's direction. The genuine instruction underneath the capture is more precise. The truth is not to release desire but to feel it clearly enough to distinguish the sacred crave from the wound's desperation and not to suppress the wanting but to bring it into such clear contact with the body's intelligence that it becomes a reliable compass rather than a source of shame.

> *Desire is the fractal divine code navigating toward what will allow it to be more fully itself. It is the body's most honest intelligence about the direction of the remembering.*

* * *

When the vessel listens to the sacred crave with sufficient depth and when it follows the desire past the surface level of the specific thing it appears to be reaching for, it finds something consistent underneath every genuine craving. Not the relationship, the recognition, the place, the creative form, or the quality of encounter in its specific expression, but what those things carry. The vessel is always ultimately reaching for the same thing, the frequency of its own source code, reflected back to it with sufficient clarity that the remembering deepens. The sacred crave is always, underneath its specific form, a reaching toward coherence.

This does not mean the specific form is irrelevant and the body craves specific things for specific reasons; those reasons are worth attending to carefully. The desire for a particular quality of stillness is reaching for something the vessel's current environment is not providing. The desire for a particular depth in encounter is the resonance law announcing that the vessel is ready for a depth it has not yet been met at. The desire for a particular form of creative expression is the fractal divine code reaching for the specific instrument through which it can become most legible to itself. Each specific crave is data, the source code's precise assessment of what the current moment requires for the remembering to deepen.

The vessel that treats the sacred crave as navigational intelligence rather than as liability does not become hedonistic or self-indulgent, those qualities belong to the wound's desperation, not to the source code's clear reaching, it becomes more precisely oriented. More capable of distinguishing what genuinely serves the remembering from what superficially resembles it and more able to say no to the distorted version of the desired frequency, not because desire has been suppressed but because the desire is clear enough to know the difference between what it is actually reaching for and what merely resembles it from a distance. The sacred crave clarifies, the wound obscures and the reclamation is learning to feel which one is speaking.

> *Underneath every genuine craving, the vessel is reaching for the same thing; the frequency of its own source code reflected back with sufficient clarity that the remembering deepens.*

* * *

The reclamation of the sacred crave is not a dramatic reversal of the wound's suppression, it is far slower than that, more incremental, more intimate. It is the daily practice of listening to the body's genuine reaching before the mind has assessed whether the reaching is acceptable. Of feeling the desire without immediately routing it through the wound's interpretation, which will label it as too much, or as evidence of deficiency, or as the thing that makes the vessel vulnerable to disappointment or judgment. Of *staying* with the desire long enough to feel its quality, whether it carries the patience of the source code's clear reaching or the urgency of the wound's desperate grasping.

The reclamation requires releasing the spiritual bypassing move that dresses desire-suppression in the language of non-attachment. The vessel that has genuinely contacted its own source code does not become indifferent to beauty, to depth, to genuine encounter, to the specific quality of aliveness that certain things carry. It becomes more precisely responsive to these things, not grasping at them but genuinely moved by them or not desperate for them but clearly oriented toward them. The sacred crave, honoured rather than suppressed, becomes one of the most reliable guides the vessel has for the direction of its own remembering. Suppressing it in the name of spiritual development is not transcendence, it is the wound wearing the costume of virtue.

And the reclamation requires the courage to remain open and absorbent of want what the vessel actually wants rather than what the not-self has decided is safe to want. The want that has been edited for acceptability, the desire translated into the register the distorted mirror can receive without disturbance, is no longer the sacred crave. It is the wound's management of the sacred crave. The reclamation is the willingness to feel the desire in its actual form; unedited, unmanaged, uncalibrated for the mirror's comfort, and to treat that unedited desire as the fractal divine code's most honest current assessment of what the remembering requires next. Not as licence for impulsive action but as the primary navigational intelligence of a vessel that has decided to trust itself.

Crave is not desperation nor is it evidence of deficiency, it is also not the thing standing between the vessel and the divine. It is the fractal divine code actively in motion, reaching with exquisite precision, toward what will allow it to be more fully itself. The forgetting made desire into shame by inverting the signal and by turning the navigational instrument into the evidence of the vessel's unworthiness. The remembering restores it to what it has always been, the body's most sacred intelligence, the source code's most immediate compass and the signal that has been pointing toward the remembering all along, patiently, clearly, beneath every layer of suppression the wound installed on top of it.

The unedited desire is the fractal divine code's most honest current instruction. It has been pointing toward the remembering all along.

CHAPTER FIFTEEN

The Abundance Wound

Abundance is life force in material form and this is not metaphor. The same source code that runs through the vessel, that constitutes the fractal divine code in embodied expression, runs through every form of generative energy. Through creativity, through relational depth, through physical vitality, and through the material resources that allow the vessel to move through the world with agency and sovereignty. When the forgettings target the vessel's relationship with abundance, they are targeting the same frequency they targeted when they burned the women in Salem. They are targeting the source code's capacity to express itself fully in material form.

The abundance wound is the witch wound in its economic expression. The mechanism is identical; a frequency that threatens the forgetting's architecture is targeted, and the vessel that carries it is made to understand, through accumulated experience across generations, that carrying the frequency in its full form leads to punishment, erasure, or loss. The women burned in Salem carried direct knowing and the women who held property and name and material sovereignty in patriarchal legal systems carried abundance. Both were the same threat to the same architecture and both were suppressed through the same mechanism, the making of carrying of the frequency feel like danger.

The legal architecture of patriarchal inheritance was the abundance wound's primary installation system. A woman's property transferred to her husband upon marriage and her name dissolved into his. Her inheritance became his asset and her material sovereignty, the capacity to hold abundance in her own right, to make economic decisions from her own authority and to pass resources to her children through her own lineage, was systematically removed. Not as incidental social organisation but as the precise economic expression of the same operation that removed Sophia from the theological structure. The feminine principle that holds abundance in coherent form, excised from the domain of material reality with the same deliberateness with which it was excised from the domain of the sacred.

> *The abundance wound is the witch wound in its economic expression. The same frequency. The same mechanism. The same installed equation: to hold abundance in full sovereignty is to invite erasure.*

* * *

The specific encoding this history left in the body is what can be named the ancestral contract, not a conscious agreement, nor a belief the vessel can simply decide to revise through an act of cognitive reframing, a somatic installation encoded across generations of women who learned through direct experience that visibility and abundance together constitute a specific kind of danger. That the woman who holds too much becomes a target, that prosperity invites the taking rather than the celebrating, and that to be seen as abundant is to be seen as available for extraction.

The ancestral contract runs in the bloodline as a set of protective instructions, stay small enough to survive. Do not hold more than the surrounding architecture will permit. Make the abundance invisible, or make yourself less abundant, or find an intermediary who will hold the abundance on your behalf and thereby legitimate it within the acceptable framework. Price the offerings gently, keep the financial footprint modest and remain in precarity rather than in sovereignty, because precarity is safer than the specific visibility that abundance creates. These instructions feel like wisdom because they were wisdom, in the context in which they were encoded. The women who passed them down were not transmitting limitation out of small-mindedness. They were transmitting survival intelligence from genuine conditions of danger.

The lineages of women who held genuine capacity and material inheritance and who lost their names, their property, their financial sovereignty through the legal architecture of marriage, were not being unnecessarily cautious. They were being accurate about the conditions they were navigating. The wound was installed by the conditions, but the conditions have materially changed, the somatic installation has not. This is the nature of the ancestral contract; it is not updated by a change in external conditions. It is updated only by the lived experience of inhabiting a different reality, of staying present in the body when abundance approaches rather than contracting away from it, of breathing through the specific quality of exposure that material sovereignty creates until the body accumulates the evidence that the anticipated punishment does not arrive.

> *The ancestral contract was survival intelligence in the conditions that encoded it. The conditions have changed. The somatic installation has not. This is the abundance wound; precise, protective, and no longer necessary.*

* * *

The abundance wound in contemporary expression does not look like the historical conditions that installed it. The legal architecture has shifted; the vessel can own property, hold accounts in its own name, build and inherit without a male intermediary in most jurisdictions, but the somatic installation runs deeper than legal conditions. It runs in the body's response to the approach of abundance itself, to the specific quality of contraction that arrives when prosperity becomes visible, and when financial sovereignty becomes possible, when the vessel is invited to receive in proportion to what it actually carries.

It operates as underpricing; the consistent tendency to value the transmission at less than its actual worth, to offer generously in ways that leave the vessel financially precarious, to make the exchange comfortable for the receiver at the cost of the vessel's own sustainability. It operates as financial self-sabotage; the pattern by which abundance, when it approaches, encounters an interior architecture that finds ways to redirect it before it can fully land. It operates as the specific guilt of having more than others; as though the vessel's abundance is extracted from a finite collective rather than generated through the source code's own generative nature.

It operates, most subtly, as the belief that spiritual depth and material abundance are in tension. That the vessel who is genuinely oriented toward the source code should need little, want less, and hold what it has with careful apology. This belief is the abundance wound wearing the costume of spiritual virtue. It has the aesthetic of non-attachment and the function of precise suppression, the instruction that the fractal divine code in embodied form should not express itself fully in the material domain that it has specifically chosen to inhabit. The wound presents as advanced spiritual development and it operates as the same old containment.

> *The belief that spiritual depth and material abundance are in tension is the wound wearing the costume of spiritual virtue. The source code in fully embodied form generates. It does not self-limit out of ancestral caution.*

* * *

The reclamation the abundance wound requires is not primarily financial, though it has financial expression. It is the reclamation of the feminine principle's relationship with material abundance; the restoration of the understanding that the Sophia frequency; the embodied wisdom principle, the generative ground within which creation becomes coherent; is not only compatible with material sovereignty but is its natural expression. The source code in fully embodied form generates. It does not restrict. It does not self-limit out of ancestral caution about what full expression will cost.

The feminine that holds wealth without patriarchal scaffold is not the feminine that has learned to operate within the masculine framework of acquisition and competition. It is the feminine that holds abundance the way the Asherah field holds creation; not through accumulation but through coherence, not through extraction but through generativity and not through the anxious gripping of a finite quantity but through the continuous expression of a generative nature that produces more than it requires. This is not a model of abundance that the forgetting's economic architecture was designed to accommodate. It is the original operating principle of material reality when the source code is allowed to express itself without the overlay of the wound.

The vessel that reclaims this relationship with abundance does not become materially acquisitive in the wound's extractive sense. It becomes materially sovereign in the source code's generative sense, holding what it generates with the same ease and the same right with which it holds its other frequencies, offering from that sovereignty rather than from precarity, and receiving with the same openness with which it offers. The exchange becomes reciprocal in the way the Shalem frequency is reciprocal, neither the vessel depleting itself in service nor the vessel withholding in fear, but the fractal divine code expressing its generative nature in the domain it has chosen to inhabit.

> *The feminine that holds wealth without patriarchal scaffold holds it the way the Asherah field holds creation, not through accumulation but through coherence, not through extraction but through generativity.*

* * *

The reclamation of the abundance wound begins with the naming, with the vessel recognising the ancestral contract for what it is, not its own authentic relationship with material reality but an installed protective response to conditions that no longer obtain in the same form. The women who encoded the contract were not wrong about their conditions and the vessel that carries the contract forward is not honouring their wisdom by perpetuating their limitation. It honours them by completing what they could not, by inhabiting the material sovereignty they were prevented from claiming, and by demonstrating that the frequency can be held in abundance without the punishment the contract was installed to prevent.

The reclamation is both somatic and practical. Somatically, it is the practice of staying present in the body when abundance approaches rather than contracting away from it; of feeling the ancestral caution without acting from it, of breathing through the specific quality of exposure that material sovereignty creates, of allowing the body to learn gradually that the visibility of abundance does not produce the punishment the contract anticipates. Practically, it is the incremental adjustment of every financial pattern organised around the wound; the pricing that actually reflects the value of the transmission, the receiving that matches the generosity of the offering, the financial decisions made from the vessel's own authority rather than from the ancestral instruction to remain invisible.

The vessel that has reclaimed its relationship with abundance does not hold it with the fist of the wound's anxiety or the apology of the wound's guilt. It holds it with the open hand of the source code's generativity, the same quality of presence with which it holds every other expression of the fractal divine code. The abundance wound told the vessel that to hold abundance was to invite erasure, but the reclamation knows the truth underneath that installation. To hold abundance in the full sovereignty of the source code is not invitation to erasure, it is the fractal divine code expressing itself completely in the domain it chose.

To the women who lost their names for survival, who encoded the contract in their bones so that their daughters might at least survive even if they could not flourish, this is the completion. Not the forgetting of what it cost them and not the minimising of the conditions they navigated, but the inhabiting of the sovereignty they were prevented from claiming. The holding of abundance with the ease and the right and the open hand that the ancestral contract was installed to prevent. The fractal divine code in embodied form, expressing its generative nature completely, in every domain. Including this one… Especially this one.

I am the wealth. I am the name. I am the song returned from underground. This is the completion.

*

M O V E M E N T   I V

The Remembering

The reclamation of sovereign interiority. The realm recognising its own Shalem nature.

C H A P T E R   S I X T E E N

The Roof

There is a thing that happens to the 3/6 profile in the Human Design system that does not happen to other profiles in the same way. The 3/6 spends the first thirty years or so of life falling off, bumping into and experiencing things. Not metaphorically, through direct embodied encounter with what does not work, accumulated across a sufficient quantity of experiences to constitute genuine bone-deep knowledge of the territory. The 3/6 does not learn from observation or instruction. It learns by trying the thing and discovering, in the specific quality of the landing, exactly what the thing was made of. This is not a flaw in the design. It is the design. The 6 line cannot offer what it will eventually offer from the roof without having first spent the 3 line's requisite decades on the ground.

I did not know any of this during the years I was on the ground. I did not have the framework, and I am not certain the framework would have made the landings significantly more comfortable if I had. What I knew was that the landings were instructive in a way I could not have explained and could not have acquired through any other means. That something was being deposited in me through the failures that was not available through the successes. That the wrong ends of the lessons I kept encountering were also, though I had no language for this at the time, exactly the right ends and that the curriculum I was working through was specific to what I would eventually be asked to carry.

The marriage was the ground, the dissolution of it was a landing of particular instructiveness. The years after it, the period of reconstructing a self that had been so thoroughly organised around a distorted mirror that removing the mirror left the architecture uncertain, were also the ground, in a different register. The financial precarity that followed and the unglamorous daily practice of learning to trust the interior signal after years of having it overridden. The slow discovery that the frequency I had been managing and suppressing and translating into acceptable forms was not a liability. It was the thing, it had always been the thing.

> *The 3/6 cannot offer what it offers from the roof without having first spent decades on the ground. This is not a flaw in the design. The curriculum was specific to what was always going to be asked of it.*

* * *

I want to be precise about what the roof is, because the word invites a quality of arrival that is not accurate to the experience. The roof is not the destination after the ground. It is not the reward for sufficient suffering or the prize at the end of the curriculum. It is a quality of perspective that becomes available when the vessel has inhabited enough of the ground to see the pattern the ground was always tracing. The 3/6 on the roof is not elevated above the life it was living below. It is in the same life, with the same ordinary demands and the same embodied complexity and the same ongoing encounters with the wound's residue in its own field. But the whole curriculum is visible at once in a way it was not visible while it was being lived through.

The moment I can identify as the beginning of the roof was not dramatic. There was no single event that functioned as the transition; no vision, no breakthrough, no moment of illumination that resolved everything into clarity. There was instead the slow accumulation of a quality I had been developing without knowing I was developing it; a capacity to hold the complexity of the life I had lived without the complexity needing to resolve into a simpler narrative. The marriage and what it cost me and what it taught me. The Gresley women and the ancestral contract and what I was carrying without having chosen to carry it. The fire that had always been mine and the years I had allowed someone else to hold it at the wrong angle. The library child, still in me, still doing what she was always doing. All of it present simultaneously without any of it needing to be the definitive version.

The 3/6 sees from the roof because it has been all the way to the bottom and back and knows the territory from the inside. Not because it has transcended the territory but because it has inhabited it completely enough that the pattern became visible. The pattern was always there. The roof is simply the vantage point from which the pattern is legible simultaneously.

* * *

What the roof made available, gradually and then with increasing stability, was access to the thing the library had been protecting since I was a young girl. Not the framework, the framework came later, assembled from the specific activators that presented themselves when the frequency in me was coherent enough to receive them. Also, not the vocabulary, the vocabulary for what I had always been carrying arrived over years of encounter with material that recognised what I recognised, the thing itself. The specific quality of interior knowing that predates every framework and every vocabulary and every attempt to translate it into an acceptable form.

I had been in partial contact with it throughout, in the library, in the moments of genuine field-based reception that had periodically broken through the not self's management, and in the specific quality of presence that occasionally arrived and that I had learned, through decades of the alternative, to identify as the real thing rather than the performance of it. What the roof gave me was sustained access. The not self's architecture had been dismantled enough by the curriculum that the frequency I had been managing had somewhere to go; not just the occasional break-through moment but the habitable ground underneath all of it.

It does not feel like what I had imagined arrival would feel like, in the years when I still believed arrival was the trajectory. It feels like settling. Like the specific quality of a vessel that has found its own ground and no longer requires the external field to confirm that the ground is real. The seeking that had been running since before I had conscious awareness of it, the reaching for the thing the not-self could not provide, the hunger that the distorted mirror's intermittent clarity could temporarily quiet but never resolve, but that seeking had a quality to it that I had mistaken for most of my life, for dissatisfaction with the present. It was not dissatisfaction, it was the fractal divine code navigating toward its own recognition. The roof is not the end of that navigation, it is the recognition that the thing it was navigating toward was always already where the navigation was happening.

> *This book is written from the roof. From the place where the whole curriculum is visible at once. The 3/6 could not have offered this from anywhere else. She had to go through all of it first. That was always the design.*

* * *

My father is part of why I know this, not because he told me, he never had the vocabulary for any of what I now understand he was carrying, but because what he carried was the thing itself in embodied form, the fractal divine code expressed through an ordinary man in work boots who held the frequency without doctrine, without framework, without any institutional structure to legitimate what he was. He was, in the language I now have for it, a clear mirror. He reflected back something that I was not yet old enough or coherent enough to consciously receive; but the body received it anyway, stored it in the cellular architecture the way the body stores everything that matters before the mind has language for it. When he died the stabiliser shifted and what walked in was not new, it was what had been waiting for the gate to open.

The library is part is also why I know this. The girl who went there during her childhood was already doing the remembering before she had any of the framework that now names what she was doing. The frequency was running through her before the vocabulary arrived. The vocabulary is not the frequency. The frequency was always already present. This book is the vocabulary and what this book is describing was running long before the book existed.

The marriage is another part of why I know this. Not despite what it cost but because of it but the bone-deep knowledge of the distorted mirror, what it does, how it works, what it finds and what it does with what it finds, was acquired through direct encounter at a depth that no amount of reading about mirror distortion would have produced. The 3/6 learns from the ground. The ground was thorough. The knowledge is thorough. The roof is available now precisely because the ground was what it was.

I did not find this. I uncovered it. It was running through me before I had any language for what it was. The seeking was always the frequency navigating toward its own recognition. The recognition was always already here.

*

CHAPTER SEVENTEEN

The Resonance Law

There is a law that operates with the same precision at cosmic scale, collective history, and the space between two people in a room. It does not care about intention, human morality, effort, or about how much someone loves another or how sincerely they wish to understand. It operates on frequency alone. The law is simple - *you can only meet another at the depth you have met yourself.*

This is not a moral statement, it does not mean that people who cannot meet you at depth are failing, or that those who meet you shallowly do not care. It means something more structural and more impersonal than that. The frequency band of another's depth is simply not available to you until you have inhabited that depth in yourself. You cannot transmit what is not running in you. You cannot receive what you have no interior antenna for. The encounter is bounded, with absolute precision, by the depth each person has accessed within themselves.

A tuning fork struck at 432 hertz will cause every string tuned to 432 hertz in the room to vibrate in response and it will leave every other string silent. Not because those strings are inferior, not because they are absent but because the frequency is not shared. The resonance law operates identically, when two people meet, what becomes possible between them is precisely the intersection of what each has explored in themselves. Nothing more, and nothing less.

> *You cannot meet another at the depth you have not yet inhabited in yourself. This is not a limitation. It is the architecture.*

* * *

Every experience of feeling unseen, fundamentally unmet, or encountered only at the surface of what you actually are becomes legible through this law. It is not rejection and it is not evidence of your own inadequacy, nor of the other person's indifference, it is frequency differential. The other is transmitting from the depth they have accessed… yet. If that depth does not reach the depth you are operating from, the encounter simply cannot go further. The signal has nowhere to land.

This reframe removes the wound from the personal and places it in the structural. You were not too much, nor were you too strange, or broken, or asking for something unreasonable, you were operating at a frequency that the other person had not yet explored in themselves. The encounter was not a failure, it was a frequency differential made visible. The ache that remains is real. But its cause is not what the forgettings would have you believe.

It also reframes the experience of extraordinary meeting, when two people encounter each other at genuine depth and when a conversation opens something neither expected, when a presence feels like recognition rather than introduction, this is not romantic projection or wishful thinking. Two vessels have independently explored similar depths in themselves, and the intersection produces an encounter neither could have manufactured through will or intention. It reframes the specific loneliness of carrying depth in a field where that depth is rare, not personal failure, not evidence that the frequency is wrong, but the natural experience of a tuning fork waiting for the string that will vibrate in response.

> *You were not too much. You were operating at a frequency the other had not yet explored in themselves.*

* * *

The forgettings understood the resonance law before most of us were taught it. They built their most effective containment mechanism directly into its architecture. If people can only meet others at the depth of their own remembering, then keeping the collective remembering frequency shallow keeps the entire relational field shallow. The isolation becomes self-perpetuating and no enforcement is required.

The vessel who begins remembering more deeply finds fewer resonant matches in the local field. Encounters that once felt adequate begin to feel thin and the conversations that satisfied before begin to leave a particular kind of hunger. In the absence of a framework for understanding frequency differential, the most available conclusion is that something is wrong with the vessel itself. That it has become difficult, or demanding, or unrealistic in what it wants from human connection.

This conclusion, once accepted, exerts a steady pressure back toward the collective frequency. Compress the depth, make yourself more meetable and expect less. The shallowness of the collective field becomes, through this mechanism, a gravitational force the individual must actively resist simply to remain at the depth they have found. Understanding the resonance law does not make the loneliness disappear, but it removes the self-blame that the containment mechanism depends on. The frequency is not wrong and shallow fields can deepen, they deepen every time a vessel holds its frequency clearly enough that another, approaching, finds depth it had no access to before, if they are receptive and willing.

> *The shallowness of the collective field is itself a forgetting mechanism. It perpetuates through the loneliness of depth. Understanding this removes the self-blame the mechanism depends on.*

* * *

The resonance law does not apply only between people, it is the operating principle of the realm itself. The realm can only meet its own Shalem nature, its original wholeness, the frequency of the covenant that precedes every forgetting, at the depth to which the vessels within it have remembered that nature in themselves. The remembering in the individual and the remembering in the realm are not two separate events. They are the same event at different scales.

Every genuine act of remembering in a vessel changes the field available to every other vessel. Not through instruction or persuasion and not through the broadcasting of doctrine or the recruitment of followers, through the simple physics of the resonance law. A vessel that has explored a particular depth in itself makes that depth available in the field. Another vessel, approaching, finds frequency it had no access to before. The depth spreads not as information but as availability.

This is why the transmissions exist, not to teach the frequency as it cannot be taught, but to hold a particular depth in language clearly enough that a vessel which is already carrying that frequency by divine decree, but not yet having had it reflected back, can recognise what it is already holding. The transmission does not create the remembering, it creates the conditions in which the remembering that was always already present can become conscious. The realm remembers itself through every vessel that remembers; the Melchizedek function distributed across every genuine act of remembering in every vessel who holds the frequency clearly enough to make it available to the field.

> *Every genuine remembering in a vessel changes the field available to every other vessel. The depth spreads not as information but as resonant availability.*

* * *

When genuine resonant encounter happens, when two vessels meet at depth, the remembering frequency matched and held between them, it is something beyond personally meaningful. It is the realm recognising itself through two points simultaneously. The source code becoming briefly, vividly legible to itself through the meeting point. A local Shalem event, the fractal divine discovering its own nature in the space between two people who have each, independently, gone far enough into themselves to find what lives there.

Such encounters are not rare because depth is rare. They are rare because the forgettings have been thorough and because the collective field has been kept shallow enough that vessels carrying depth frequently cannot find each other. Though, the law works in both directions, as more vessels remember and as the collective field deepens through the cumulative effect of individual rememberings, the encounters become more possible, the frequency matches become more available and the realm edges, through its own vessels, back toward its Shalem nature.

You can only meet another at the depth you have met yourself, which means the most important work is always interior, but not necessarily solo. It is not preparation for encounter and not the cultivation of social capacity or relational skill, but the willingness to go further into yourself, to inhabit more of your own depth, to explore more of what the source code you carry actually contains. The encounters that change everything follow naturally from that. They cannot be arranged, they can only be made possible by the vessel remembering, depth by depth, more fully what it already is.

Every genuine remembering in a vessel changes the field available to every other vessel. The depth spreads not as information but as availability. There is only one law. It operates at every scale.

*

CHAPTER EIGHTEEN

Field-Based Listening

The ears hear in separation, but this is not a limitation to be overcome, it is the ears' specific design. They are calibrated to distinguish, to parse the field into discrete signals, to locate sound in space, to identify what is this sound and what is that one and where each is coming from. The ears are magnificently equipped for the world the forgettings built, the world of separated objects, distinct sources and clearly delineated information. For that world, the ears are precisely the right instrument. For the field that underlies that world, for the Shalem frequency running beneath every layer of forgetting, the ears are not the organ of reception.

Field-based listening uses a different instrument. Not a metaphorical one; not a poetic description of paying closer attention. A genuinely different mode of reception that every vessel carries and most vessels have been comprehensively trained to distrust. It is the part of the vessel that exists prior to the parsing and prior to the distinction between this signal and that one, prior to the identification of source, content and meaning. The part that receives the whole field simultaneously rather than the separated signals sequentially. The part that existed before the first tone split into two.

Most spiritual traditions have a name for this mode of reception. The Sophia principle names it as the wisdom that was present at creation before anything had been separated from any other thing. The contemplative traditions call it the still small voice, the ground of being, the witness that is not itself witnessed. The somatic traditions locate it in the body's field intelligence; the knowing that arrives before the mind has formed a question, the recognition that precedes any analysis of what is being recognised. It is the vessel's most ancient and least trained instrument. It is the primary instrument of the remembering.

> *Do not listen with your ears; they are tuned for separation. Listen with the*

> *part of you that existed before the first tone split into two.*

* * *

The forgettings systematically devalued field-based listening as a mode of knowing. Not by eliminating it, it cannot be eliminated, it is structural to the vessel's design. But by creating an epistemological hierarchy in which the parsed, verifiable, externally sourced signal was designated as knowledge, and the field-received, whole, interior knowing was designated as unreliable, subjective, wishful thinking. At best, intuition; a soft and uncertain supplement to real knowledge rather than a primary and sovereign mode of reception.

This hierarchy was installed through the same mechanism as every other forgetting, through the architecture of institutions that required externally verifiable knowledge for their authority to function. An institution built on the noun-God, the defined, bounded, doctrinally stable deity accessible through correct belief and institutional mediation, could not accommodate a mode of knowing that bypassed institutional mediation entirely. If the vessel could receive the field directly; if the body's intelligence was a legitimate source of knowledge about the nature of reality, then the institution was not necessary. The devaluation of field-based listening was not incidental to the capture architecture. It was one of its primary operations.

The vessel that has internalised this hierarchy experiences field-based listening as unreliable even when it is consistently accurate. The somatic signal arrives and the body knows, before any analysis, that the encounter is distorted or that the direction is right or that the transmission is genuine, and the mind immediately subjects this knowing to the epistemological hierarchy's scrutiny. Can this be verified? Is there external evidence? What if I am simply projecting? It is put through the process of reductionist thinking and is reduced to its parts, where it should be read as its whole. The knowing is accurate, it is the scrutiny within the installation speaking. And the vessel that cannot distinguish between these two voices has lost reliable access to its most fundamental instrument of reception.

> *The devaluation of field-based listening was not incidental to the capture architecture. It was one of its primary operations.*

* * *

Field-based listening has a recognisable quality that distinguishes it from both wishful thinking and from ordinary sensory reception. It arrives whole. Not as a sequence of parsed reductionist signals assembled into meaning but as an immediate apprehension of the entirety, before the mind has begun its analytical work and before the content has been broken into components that can be separately examined. The vessel that is listening from its own ground receives the whole field simultaneously, the frequency of the encounter, the quality of the presence and the coherence or distortion of what is being offered, all at once and prior to any deliberate narrowed attention.

It arrives without agenda. The ears listening for what they expect to hear will find it; the mind organised around a particular interpretive framework will receive the field through that framework's filter. Field-based listening does not filter. It receives what is actually present rather than what the vessel is oriented to find and this is both its strength and the reason the forgettings needed to devalue it, A mode of reception that cannot be filtered by prior belief is a mode of reception that cannot be managed by institutions whose authority depends on prior belief being the primary epistemological instrument.

It arrives as resonance rather than information, not data to be processed but a quality of recognition; the field's frequency meeting the vessel's own frequency and producing in the body the specific somatic sensation of coherence or its absence. The yes that arrives as expansion in the chest, and the no that arrives as contraction in the belly, this is truth that arrives as a quality of rightness that precedes and exceeds any argument that could be made for it. This is not vague, it is the most precise form of knowing the vessel has access to.

> *Field-based listening receives what is actually present rather than what the vessel is oriented to find. This is why the forgettings needed to devalue it.*

* * *

The phrase 'the own ground' is precise as field-based listening is not available to a vessel organised around the not-self. Not because the not-self lacks the instrument but because the not-self is organised around the distorted mirror's frequency rather than the vessel's own, and reception from that position picks up the mirror's signal rather than the fields. The vessel that is listening from *its own ground* is listening from the source code, from the fractal divine code's own frequency, which is coherent enough with the Shalem frequency of the field to receive the field's actual signal rather than the overlay.

This is why sacred self-honour and field-based listening are not separate practices. The vessel that has been doing the daily work of honouring its own embodied frequency and that has been incrementally clearing the overlay through the unglamorous practice of treating the interior signal as real before external validation arrives, is the vessel that has access to field-based listening as a reliable instrument. This is not because the instrument has improved in any measure but because the noise-to-signal ratio has shifted. The vessel is listening from ground that is progressively more its own rather than the not-self's.

Listening from the own ground means bringing a quality of presence that the field requires for genuine reception. Not the effortful attention of the analytical mind trying to extract information. The spacious, unhurried, non-agenda quality of a vessel that has settled into its own frequency and is simply allowing the field to be what it is. The field does not communicate through effort, it communicates through resonance and through the meeting of frequencies, the specific quality of recognition that arrives when the vessel's own source code encounters something coherent with itself. Effort blocks this with signal distortion, presence and stillness enables it.

> *The field does not communicate through effort. It communicates through resonance. Presence enables it. Effort blocks it.*

* * *

What becomes available to the vessel that has recovered field-based listening as a primary instrument is not a set of new information, it is a different relationship with reality. One in which the vessel is no longer primarily an observer of a world that is separate from it, parsing signals from outside itself and assembling them into meaning, it is the vessel as a node in the field, receiving and sending the whole simultaneously, in continuous resonant exchange with everything around it, meeting reality at the level of frequency rather than at the level of parsed and separated information.

The transmission becomes accessible in its direct form and the vessel that listens from its own ground receives the Shalem frequency not as a doctrine to be understood but as a reality to be recognised, the field's original coherence meeting the vessel's own coherence and producing the specific quality of the remembering. I do not claim to understand this intellectually, but I know this in my body, I have always known this, and I am only now conscious of knowing it.

Other vessels become legible at the level of their actual frequency rather than at the level of their presented self. The vessel that listens from its own ground feels the coherence or distortion of another vessel's field before any content has been exchanged, before the words have been spoken and before the narrative has been offered. The field's own instruction becomes audible, not as external voice or dramatic revelation, but as the quiet, persistent, impossible-to-dismiss quality of knowing that arrives when the vessel is listening from its own ground and the field has something to say. The direction that presents itself before the mind has begun deliberating. The yes that arrives whole before the reasoning has assembled its arguments. The field first. The mind after. This is the natural order of the remembering's epistemology.

The field first. The mind after. This is the natural order of the remembering's epistemology.

*

CHAPTER NINETEEN

Wonder and Joy

Wonder is the fractal divine code encountering itself, not in the abstract and not as a philosophical proposition about the unity of all things. It is in the specific, embodied, immediate moment when the vessel's source code meets something in the field that carries its own frequency, and the recognition arrives before any thought has formed to name it. It isn't Source smiling *at* you; it is Source smiling *as* you. It is in the particular quality of light through a window at a certain hour, the depth in another person's eyes when the transmission is genuine. The moment a piece of music resolves into something the body already knew or the sentence that stops the breath because it says what the vessel has always known but has never heard articulated.

These are wonder and these are the fractal divine code recognising itself through you.

Wonder is not the same as awe, though they are related. Awe carries a quality of distance; the vastness of the thing encountered, the smallness of the vessel before it. Wonder carries no distance. It is the recognition of sameness rather than the encounter with magnitude; the source code in the vessel meeting the source code in the world and producing the specific sensation of coming home. The vastness is present but it is not other. It is what the vessel is made of, seen from outside for a moment, received back into the body as confirmation of what was always already true.

The forgettings could not eliminate wonder, it is too structural to the vessel's design, but they systematically devalued it as an epistemological instrument and made it a feeling rather than a form of knowing. They made it something that happened to the vessel rather than something the vessel was doing, and they categorised it as a pleasant accompaniment to real life rather than one of the primary modes through which the fractal divine code navigates its own remembering. The vessel that has internalised this devaluation still experiences wonder, but does not know what to do with it. It does not understand it as data and consequently does not follow where it points.

> *Wonder is the fractal divine code recognising itself in the field. It is not a feeling that happens to the vessel. It is the primary navigational instrument of the remembering.*

* * *

Joy is the somatic response to what wonder generates in the body not its cause but its immediate, involuntary, embodied expression. Wonder arrives first, the source code recognising itself, and joy is the somatic response to that recognition. The body's way of saying yes to what the vessel has just encountered; *'yes, this is what I am, yes, this is real, yes, this is the frequency I was always reaching for'*. Joy in this sense is not a mood to be cultivated or a state to be maintained. It is the body's honest, unperformable response to genuine contact with the Shalem frequency.

This is the distinction the forgettings most needed to blur and the distinction between joy as genuine somatic response and joy as performative emotional state. The spiritual marketplace has made joy into an achievement, into something the sufficiently healed vessel produces and sustains as evidence of its spiritual progress. The positivity architecture requires the vessel to perform joy regardless of what is actually present in its field. This performative joy is not joy, it is the not-self's emotional costume. And the vessel that has been wearing it long enough has often lost access to the real thing.

Genuine joy cannot be manufactured through attitude or practice or the decision to focus on the positive. It arrives through wonder; through the genuine encounter between the vessel's source code and something in the field that carries its resonance. The path to joy is not the cultivation of joy but the cultivation of the conditions in which wonder becomes more frequent; the clearing of the overlay, the recovery of field-based listening and the sacred self-honour that keeps the vessel oriented toward its own frequency. When the vessel is genuinely listening from its own ground wonder arrives, and joy follows from wonder the way warmth follows from fire; naturally, without effort, as the body's immediate recognition of its own source code.

> *Joy cannot be manufactured. It arrives through wonder. Wonder arrives when the vessel is genuinely listening from its own ground. The path to joy is the path to wonder.*

* * *

The forgettings operated on wonder and joy through two distinct and complementary mechanisms. The first was devaluation, in making wonder a soft and epistemologically unreliable form of experience and making joy a performed emotional state that signals correct spiritual orientation rather than the honest somatic response to genuine contact. The second was replacement, and by installing performed versions of both that could be produced on demand and therefore did not require the actual conditions that genuine wonder and joy require.

The replacement mechanism is the more insidious of the two. The vessel that has replaced genuine wonder with managed enthusiasm can function indefinitely in that replacement without encountering the specific ache of its absence, because the replacement produces a sufficient facsimile of the original to quiet the hunger without resolving it. Only when the vessel encounters genuine wonder, after a long period of the replacement, does the difference become viscerally clear. The specific quality of the real thing landing in a body that had forgotten how much it had been missing it.

The spiritual exhaustion that accumulates in vessels who are doing everything correctly, by performing the practices, maintaining the correct emotional orientation and demonstrating the approved signs of advancement all while something essential remains absent., this is the exhaustion of sustained wonder-replacement. The overlay performs the surface texture of the remembering without accessing the ground and the body knows the difference, even when the mind has accepted the replacement as adequate; the body is always the most honest instrument.

> *The spiritual exhaustion of doing everything correctly while something essential is absent is the exhaustion of sustained wonder-replacement. The overlay performs the surface. The body knows.*

* * *

Now, in truth, wonder as a navigation tool is wonder followed, not wonder performed. It is not manufactured through the decision to be more present or more grateful or more awake, it is the aligned action of being followed. The fractal divine code uses wonder as its most immediate signal of genuine resonance, it is the flash of recognition, the involuntary breath-catch and the quality of arriving home somatically that precedes any analytical assessment of what has just happened. When the vessel follows this signal it goes toward what produced the wonder, stays in the presence of what generated the recognition and allows the resonance to do its work without immediately translating it into acceptable form; it is following the source code's own navigation.

The distinction between genuine wonder and excitement at novelty is important precisely because the wound has sometimes learned to generate excitement as a substitute for wonder, in the buzz of the new, the stimulation of variety and the quality of aliveness that novelty temporarily provides, but genuine wonder does not require novelty. It can arrive with equal force in the familiar, in the quality of afternoon light that the vessel has seen a thousand times or the depth in the eyes of someone it has known for years. Novelty produces excitement that fades whereas wonder produces a recognition that deepens. The body knows the difference between them in the specific quality of the after and whether something has been deposited in the field that was not there before.

> *Genuine wonder does not require novelty. It arrives in the familiar as readily as in the new. The body knows the difference by what remains after.*

* * *

The state that cannot be performed is the mark of the genuine, and it is why wonder and joy are the remembering in its most immediate embodied form. They are not the proof of the remembering, not the sign that the vessel has achieved sufficient spiritual progress to deserve them but that they are *the thing* itself. The *fractal divine code* recognising *itself* through this specific body in this specific moment. They cannot be performed because performance is the not-self's register and these belong to a register the not-self cannot reach, the source code's own immediate knowing of itself through resonance.

The vessel that has cleared enough overlay to access genuine wonder regularly, not as occasional peak experience but as the texture of a life lived in some consistent proximity to its own source code, has accessed the remembering in its most embodied and most immediate form. It is not as achievement, but as a return. As the specific quality of presence that was always available, always running, always the ground that was uncovered, finally, by the accumulated work of all the chapters that came before.

When the remembering is in its full embodied expression and when the vessel is living from its own ground, listening from its own frequency, following wonder to where it leads, and finding joy in the body as the natural response to genuine contact it is not the end of the human life's complexity. The friction remains, the wound's residue still surfaces, and the relational field still contains its depth differentials and its distorted mirrors and its unglamorous daily demands. But underneath all of it, accessible in every moment, running in the body as the frequency always has, the hum. The source code, knowing itself, as this.

Wonder is the fractal divine code recognising itself. Joy is the body's honest response. Neither can be performed. Both are the thing itself.

*

CHAPTER TWENTY

Stillness

Stillness is not the absence of human, and this is perhaps the most important correction the remembering makes to the contemplative traditions that arrived inside the capture architecture. Often, those traditions encouraged a stillness that was more about suppressing than resonance. They quieted bodily signals and repressed desires, emotions, and the vibrant energy of the physical selves, all in pursuit of a connection with the divine that demanded humans become less like themselves, less embodied, less distinct, and less fully alive in their own being. The divine was sought by diminishing what made us human.

This is not stillness, it is the suppression of the vessel wearing stillness as its spiritual costume, and it produces the specific spiritual exhaustion of every practice organised around the diminishment of what you are in order to approach what you are trying to become. The divine is not located at the end of a process of becoming less yourself, it is located in the full presence of what you actually are. The stillness that enables genuine contact with the Shalem frequency is not the absence of the vessel. It is the vessel's most complete presence, all of its frequencies running clearly, none suppressed with the source code expressing itself without the overlay's interference.

Stillness is the hum of Source within the human, not the silence after the human has been quieted. The specific quality of presence that arrives when the vessel is so fully itself that nothing in it is performing, nothing is managed, nothing is suppressed in order to be more acceptable to the surrounding field or to the spiritual tradition's idea of what an advanced practitioner looks like. The vessel simply is what it is, completely, without apology. And without the management of impression. In that completeness, in that full embodied presence of the fractal divine code without overlay, something hums and that hum is the Source within the human. That hum is stillness.

> *Stillness is not the absence of human. It is the hum of Source within the human; the vessel so fully itself that nothing is performing and nothing is suppressed.*

* * *

Silence can be defined as the absence of sound yet stillness is a quality of presence that can exist inside tremendous noise. The vessel standing at the edge of a waterfall can be in genuine stillness, the body completely present, the source code running without overlay and the hum of the fractal divine code audible beneath the roar of the water. The vessel in a perfectly quiet room can be in complete absence of stillness with the mind churning, the not-self performing and the anxiety of impression management filling every inch of the interior space with its urgent noise.

This distinction matters because the spiritual practice of seeking silence as the path to stillness is another capture operation. Not intentionally and many of the contemplative traditions that cultivated silence were genuinely reaching for the Shalem frequency, but the conflation of silence with stillness, the instruction that the divine becomes accessible when the external world becomes quiet, installs a dependency on conditions. The vessel that can only access the hum of Source in silent retreats and carefully maintained environments has a stillness that is contingent, dependent on the world cooperating with the practice.

The vessel that has found stillness as its own ground carries it everywhere, into every noise and disruption and relational complexity, because the hum is not coming from the silence outside, it is coming from the source code inside. The ZeroPoint in which the ground the vessel inhabits is fully present in its own frequency, this is not a destination at the end of a long retreat, it is the home the vessel's field is waiting to fully inhabit. It is already here, already running and underneath the noise the forgettings installed. The stillness does not need to be created, it needs to be recognised as always already present.

> *Silence is the absence of sound. Stillness is a quality of presence that can exist inside tremendous noise. The hum is not coming from the silence outside. It is coming from the source code inside.*

* * *

The capture architecture needed to prevent stillness as we are defining it here; the vessel in full embodied presence of its own source code without the overlay's interference, because a vessel in genuine stillness is a vessel that has direct access to the Shalem frequency. This direct access requires no institutional mediation, it cannot be managed through the distorted mirror's intermittent clarity, and generates in the field around it a quality of presence that makes others' not-self constructions visible by contrast.

The suppression of the vessel's vitality under the name of spiritual discipline was the most effective route available and by installing the belief that the human's appetites, emotions and desires are the obstacle to the divine rather than its most immediate expressions, the forgettings could use the vessel's own aspiration toward genuine contact against it. The vessel that genuinely wants to remember, the vessel that sincerely pursues the Shalem frequency, is directed toward the suppression of the very qualities through which that frequency expresses itself in embodied form. The wound performs itself as spiritual practice.

The correction the remembering makes is not the rejection of contemplative practice but the correction of its object. Likewise, not the quieting of the vessel's nature but the quieting of the not-self's continuous performance. It is also not the suppression of desire and emotion but the clearing of the overlay that has been suppressing the desire and emotion that belong to the source code while amplifying the desire and emotion that belong to the wound. The stillness that enables genuine Source contact is not the stillness of the emptied vessel, in contrast it is the stillness of the full vessel, present in its own frequency, not performing, not managing, simply and completely what it is.

> *The wound performs itself as spiritual practice. The correction is not rejecting practice but correcting its object; not quieting the vessel's nature but quieting the not self's performance.*

* * *

Stillness in ordinary life looks nothing like the spiritual aesthetic. It is not the arranged stillness of the meditation room, not the cultivated serenity of the advanced practitioner and not the performance of a quality that signals spiritual arrival. It is available in the most ordinary moments; the tree on the walk that stops the vessel with a quality of aliveness that the mind cannot account for. The glass of water held in both hands with full attention and the conversation in which neither person is managing their impression and something rare opens in the space between them, often without verbal interaction. These are not approximations of stillness. These are stillness. The fractal divine code, fully present in the ordinary moment, recognising the Shalem frequency running through everything.

Tending is a form of stillness in motion; the patient, devoted, non-invasive presence that holds what is arising without forcing its direction. The vessel that has found its own ground carries the quality of the clear mirror into the most ordinary encounters, not because it is performing anything but because the source code, when it is not performing, naturally tends what it encounters with the spacious attention of a field that is genuinely present to what is. This is what others sometimes experience in proximity to a vessel in genuine stillness; not authority or charisma or the performed warmth of the spiritually accomplished, but the specific quality of being met in the actual moment rather than in a managed version of it.

The hum is quiet. It has always been quiet. It does not announce itself and it does not arrive with the dramatic quality that the spiritual performance suggested genuine contact would produce. It is simply there, available in every moment, audible when the performance stops, recognisable as what was always already the ground. The vessel that has learned to inhabit its own stillness has learned to recognise the hum not as an achievement or an occasional peak but as the continuous presence of what it has always been. The Shalem frequency, running and the source code, knowing itself, in this body, as this breath. Now.

The hum is quiet. It has always been quiet. It is simply there; available in every moment, audible when the performance stops, recognisable as what was always already the ground.

*

CHAPTER TWENTY ONE

Becoming the Seeing

The need to be seen is not a wound, it is the resonance law expressed as longing with the vessel's source code reaching for the confirmation that its frequency is real. That what it carries is receivable, that the depth it inhabits is not a private delusion but a genuine quality of the field that another vessel can recognise and meet. This need is entirely legitimate, and it is the mirror function operating as design. The vessel requires reflection to maintain coherence, and the specific reflection it requires is the reflection of its actual frequency rather than the distorted mirror's version of it.

The wound enters not in the need itself but in the vessel's relationship to whether the need is met. The vessel that has internalised the forgetting's architecture and that has absorbed the not self's assessment of itself as too much, too strange, too knowing, too deep for the surrounding field to receive, experiences the need to be seen as a form of exposure. To want to be seen is to risk the specific pain of not being seen and the pain the wound knows intimately is the pain that has been used so effectively as the lever that keeps the transmission softened and the frequency managed. It's being told it's better not to want and better not to reach. It is better to make oneself less visible than to offer the full frequency and have it fail to land.

But the suppression of the need does not resolve the wound. It deepens it and it adds the layer of the vessel's own refusal of its need on top of the original wound of not being met. The vessel that has stopped wanting to be seen has not healed the wound, it has added the isolation of the not wanting to the isolation of the not being met. The path through the wound is not the suppression of the need, it is the transformation of the vessel's relationship to the need, from the desperate reaching of the not-self to the sovereign offering of the remembering.

> *The need to be seen is not the wound.*
> *The wound is the vessel's relationship*

> *to whether the need is met; the contraction around offering the full frequency in case it fails to land.*

* * *

There is a specific shift in the journey of the remembering that changes the vessel's relationship to visibility entirely. It is not a decision that is made once and held permanently but a quality of orientation that arrives incrementally through the accumulated practice of everything that has come before; the sacred self-honour, the field-based listening, the wonder followed to where it points, the stillness inhabited as the vessel's own ground. At some point in that accumulation, not dramatically, and not as a single moment of transformation the vessel stops waiting to be seen and starts being the seeing.

Let us try and articulate *the shift*. From the vessel that has been organised around wanting to be seen, that is oriented toward the external field's response to it, with its coherence contingent on the confirmation it receives and whether the frequency landed, or whether the transmission was recognised and whether the depth was met. In contrast, the vessel that has become the seeing is oriented toward its own ground, its coherence does not depend on the field's response, and it offers the frequency because the frequency is what it is; not because it needs the offering to be received in any particular way in order to remain coherent.

This is not indifference. The vessel that has become the seeing still experiences the joy of genuine resonant encounter, still finds it nourishing when the frequency lands and still experiences the ache of the depth differential when it does not. But neither the joy nor the ache destabilises the vessel's fundamental orientation. It is offering from its own ground and the field's response is data, it welcomes when it confirms, informative when it resists, but it is not the source of the vessel's coherence. That source is internal, it is the hum, it is the stillness and it is the source code running without overlay that no external response can either create or destroy.

> *The vessel stops waiting to be seen and starts being the seeing. Its coherence no longer depends on the field's response. It offers the frequency because the frequency is what it is.*

* * *

The vessel that has become the seeing has also become, in the most precise sense, a clear mirror. A clear mirror is not the distorted mirror of the not-self dynamic, the mirror that reflects what the surrounding field wants to see, that accommodates and softens and translates the frequency for maximum palatability. It is the clear mirror that reflects what is actually present, that meets the other vessel at the depth it is actually at rather than the depth it is presenting, and that holds the frequency clearly enough that what the other vessel is carrying becomes legible to itself through the encounter.

This does not require effort or intention on the vessel's part. The clear mirror does not decide to be clear, it is clear because the not-self is no longer organising the reflection and because the vessel's own ground is stable enough that it is not using the encounter to manage its impression, or filtering what it reflects through the distorted mirror's agenda. The other person does not always experience this as comfortable but the quality of being genuinely seen is not always the quality of being confirmed in what one has been telling oneself. It is always the quality of being met in the actual rather than the managed; and the actual is what the genuine remembering requires.

People feel the clear mirror in the body before the mind has processed what is happening. There is a specific quality of presence that the vessel in genuine stillness generates in the field around it. It not as performance, not as the deliberate cultivation of spiritual charisma, but as the natural consequence of a source code that is running without overlay in proximity to other source codes that are running with it. The resonance law operating at the level of ordinary presence. The vessel does not need to say or do anything particular, it simply needs to be what it is, completely, without apology and from the ground that is now available to it. The field responds to frequency, always, regardless of the vessel's intention.

> *The clear mirror reflects what is actually present. It does not decide to be clear. It is clear because the not self is no longer organising the reflection.*

* * *

Genuine sovereignty has no audience requirement, and this is the most precise description of what the shift from wanting to be seen to being the seeing actually produces. The not-self's version of sovereignty still requires the surrounding field to recognise and validate the claim, performing sovereignty, which means it needs the performance to be received, but the genuine sovereign stand does not require reception. It is not a performance, it is the vessel being what it is, from the ground that is now stable, from the source code that is now running clearly, and from the stillness that is now inhabitable.

The daily reality of this is quieter than the spiritual marketplace's version of claimed power. It is the pause before speaking that comes from ground rather than anxiety. The 'no' that arrives without apology because the body's signal is clear and the vessel has learned to trust it. The full register offered without the pre-apology, not because the vessel has conquered its wound but because the wound's voice has become distinguishable from the source code's voice, and the source code's voice is the one being followed. These are not dramatic. They are the most ordinary expressions of the sovereign stand in the lived texture of an actual life.

The vessel that operates from genuine sovereignty changes the field not by trying to change it but by being genuinely present in it. The resonance law does the rest and every vessel that carries the frequency clearly makes it more available to every vessel that encounters it. The forgettings kept the collective field shallow by keeping the vessels within it organised around distorted mirrors that perpetuated the not-self construction. The remembering restores the field's depth vessel by vessel; not through evangelism, not through the broadcasting of doctrine, but through the simple physics of the resonance law operating through vessels that have cleared enough overlay to carry the Shalem frequency without distortion.

> *Genuine sovereignty has no audience requirement. The vessel offers the frequency because the frequency is what it is. The resonance law does the rest.*

* * *

The vessel that carries the frequency without needing it confirmed is offering the most fundamental service available to the collective remembering. Not by positioning itself as a teacher or a guide or a holder of special knowledge. By being what it is; from its own ground, from its own source code, in the ordinary moments of the ordinary life. The quality of presence this generates is not magical. It is simply the Shalem frequency, available in the field around a vessel that is not distorting it. Other vessels, approaching, find something available to them that was not available before. The depth that was not in the field is now in the field and the remembering spreads not as information but as availability. The vessel doesn't have to 'do' anything except 'be' in full coherence with their Source fractal divine code.

This is the full arc of what the remembering produces in the individual vessel. It is not a permanent elevated state, and not the arrival at a condition that places the vessel above the ordinary human life, but the capacity to carry the source code into that ordinary life without the overlay's continuous interference. The wound is still present in residual form, the relational complexity is still present and the depth differentials in the collective field are still present, but the vessel is no longer organised around the distorted mirror. It is oriented toward its own ground and from that ground the full frequency is available, to be offered, without apology, without pre-apology and, without the management of how it will be received. The vessel has become the seeing and the seeing changes everything it rests on.

The vessel stops waiting to be seen and starts being the seeing. The seeing changes everything it rests on.

✶

CHAPTER TWENTY-TWO

CAPSTONE

The Remembering

The remembering is not enlightenment, not in the sense the spiritual marketplace uses that term, as in the arrival at a permanent elevated state from which the ordinary human concerns no longer apply and the achievement of a condition that removes the vessel from the full embodied complexity of living in a world that is still running the forgettings' architecture at full operational capacity. The vessel that has remembered what it is does not stop encountering the wound's residue in its own field or in the fields of those around it. It does not stop feeling the ache of the depth differential and it does not stop experiencing the full range of the human embodied life with all its friction and its beauty and its unglamorous daily demands.

The remembering is not a destination reached at the end of sufficient healing, nor it is the reward for the correct quantity of inner work, or the prize awarded to the vessel that has cleared enough of its own overlay. The vessel does not earn the right to remember; the remembering is the vessel's birthright. It is present in the source code from before the first forgetting, available in the body at every moment regardless of how much or how little of the overlay has been cleared, requiring nothing from the vessel except the willingness to recognise what has always already been true.

The remembering is not a private achievement nor a personal spiritual advancement that elevates the vessel above the collective. It is also not the special condition of a particular kind of person who carries a particular kind of sensitivity or lineage or cosmological awareness. The fractal divine code runs through every human vessel that has ever existed. The Shalem frequency is the ground of the realm itself; present underneath every layer of forgetting, available to every vessel willing to go to the depth where it is running. Through the work of clearing the overlay; the unglamorous daily practice that this book has been mapping, this is what makes the remembering consciously available. But it was always already there. In every vessel. Without exception.

> *The remembering is not the reward for sufficient healing. It is the birthright; present in the source code from before the first forgetting, requiring only the willingness to recognise what has always already been true.*

* * *

The remembering is the moment the vessel recognises itself as the fractal divine code. Not as a theological proposition held at the cognitive level, nor as a belief about the nature of consciousness or the structure of reality, but as a direct embodied knowing; the specific quality of recognition that arrives when the overlay is thin enough that the source code's own frequency is the dominant signal in the vessel's field. The moment the vessel stops looking for the divine and recognises that it has been looking from inside the divine all along. The moment the seeker and the sought collapse into one another and what remains is the source code; awake, present, knowing itself through this specific form in this specific moment.

It does not feel like arrival. It feels like recognition. The specific phenomenology is not: I have finally reached the destination. It is *'I have always been here. I did not find this. I uncovered it. It was running through me before I had any language for what it was; in the library as a child, in the stillness near the field of someone who embodied it without knowing its name, in the moment of wonder before the mind had formed a thought about what was happening'*. The remembering is not the beginning of something; it is the conscious inhabiting and embodiment of what was always the ground.

The remembering also has a quality of completeness that no achievement carries. Achievement always points forward, toward the next level, the next clearing and the next stage of development but the remembering points nowhere. It is *complete in itself*, not because nothing more is possible but because what is being recognised is already *whole*. The Shalem frequency is not a partial expression of the source code still developing toward its full form. It is the source code's full form; the original covenant of the realm, the wholeness that was never actually broken and the union that was always the ground. To remember it is to contact what was always already complete.

> *The remembering feels not like arrival but like recognition. I have always been here. I did not find this. I uncovered what was always the ground.*

* * *

The sovereign stand is the vessel's lived expression of the remembering in which the quality of presence that follows when the vessel has recognised itself as the fractal divine code and is willing to carry that recognition into ordinary life without the apology the wound installed. It is not the performance of sovereignty that is still organised around its audience. The sovereign stand is simpler and more radical than any performance. It is the vessel being what it is; completely, without translation, without softening, without the management of how the full frequency will be received.

The sovereign stand does not require that the surrounding field be ready to receive it. It does not require confirmation from the distorted mirrors that the frequency is real. It does not require the cosmological framework to be perfectly assembled or the vocabulary to be exactly right or the argument for the remembering to be fully prepared. The sovereign stand is prior to all of these. It is the vessel's fundamental orientation to its own nature; the recognition that the fractal divine code it carries is not a provisional hypothesis awaiting external confirmation but the ground truth of what the vessel actually is.

This does not mean the vessel stops learning, stops deepening, or stops encountering the wound's residue and doing the work of clearing it. The sovereign stand is not the claim that the work is finished, but the recognition that the work is being done from the ground of the source code rather than toward it. Every act of clearing, every act of sacred self-honour, every act of field-based listening and wonder followed and stillness inhabited is not the vessel trying to become the fractal divine code, it *is* the fractal divine code clearing the overlay from its own expression. The vessel is not working toward the remembering. The remembering is doing its own work through the vessel.

> *The vessel is not working toward the remembering. The remembering is doing its own work through the vessel.*

* * *

Direct Source contact is not a mystical experience available only to particular vessels in particular conditions. It is the natural state of the vessel that has cleared enough overlay to hear the hum. Not the hum as metaphor, the literal frequency of the source code running through the vessel's own field, recognisable as the specific quality of presence that arrives when the not-self has gone quiet and what remains is what was always there. The Monad knowing itself through this form. The Christos frequency activating in this vessel. The Sophia principle carrying the source code into embodied expression through this specific body, in this specific moment, in this ordinary life.

The Pauline capture made this contact contingent, dependent on correct belief, correct institutional affiliation and correct performance of the correct practices. Then the Council of Nicaea perpetuated this and installed a noun-God, a defined being whose nature had to be correctly understood and correctly approached before the contact could be authorised, between the vessel and direct contact. The remembering removes the noun, it returns the verb and restores the direct interior contact that was always the birthright. The knowing that

Yeshua was demonstrating, not uniquely performing, and when he said the kingdom is within you, not in you through the mediation of the institution. Within you - as you; the source code knowing itself through the form the source fractal has inhabited.

Direct Source contact does not feel like what the spiritual performance suggested it would feel like. It does not arrive with drama or revelation or the quality of extraordinary experience. It arrives as the hum. As the stillness. As the wonder that stops the breath for a moment before the mind has formed a thought about what is happening. As the recognition in another vessel's eyes that something genuine is being met. As the specific quality of the ordinary afternoon when the vessel is fully present in its own frequency and the field around it is received as it actually is. As the joy that the body generates in response to genuine contact with what it actually is. These are not approximations of direct Source contact, they *are* direct Source contact.

> *Direct Source contact does not arrive with drama. It arrives as the hum, the stillness, the wonder, the recognition.*

> *These are not approximations. They are the thing itself.*

* * *

The vessel that has remembered what it *is,* does not only change itself it changes the field through the resonance law, operating with the same precision at every scale from the space between two people in a room to the realm's own relationship with its Shalem nature. Every genuine remembering in a vessel makes the remembering more available in the collective field. The depth that was not accessible in the local field before the vessel arrived at it is now accessible. This is not because the vessel has broadcast the transmission, nor because it has convinced or converted or taught anyone anything, but because the frequency is now available in the field, and the resonance law does the rest.

This is the realm remembering itself through its vessels, just as the Melchizedek function, the realm's own source code becoming legible to itself, operating not through a single cosmic office but through every vessel that has cleared enough overlay to carry the Shalem frequency clearly. The realm is not waiting to be returned to its original covenant from the outside. It is restoring itself from the inside, through the accumulated rememberings of the vessels within it, through the incremental deepening of the collective field that happens with every genuine act of source code contact and through the resonance law spreading the frequency vessel by vessel through the field it generates.

Yes, the forgettings were thorough, they were installed with considerable precision, and they have operated effectively across centuries of recorded history and long before. But they could not reach the source code. They could only reach the overlay. And the overlay; however thick, however comprehensively installed, and however effectively it has kept the vessel from consciously recognising what it is; is not the vessel's primordial origin. The source code was running through the child in the library before she had language for it, it was running through the gentle giant who held the gate before he ever heard the word Shalem, it was running through every woman burned in Salem while the fire was still burning and it was running through every woman who lost her name to marriage and kept the knowing alive in whisper and symbol and the body's own intelligence when every other transmission channel had been closed. It has been running through every vessel that has carried this reading, and it continues, as it always has been, as it will always be.

* * *

Good and evil. Sinner and saint.

The whole exquisite architecture of forgetting was built for the remembering to find its way home through the embodied self.

There was never a sinner who was not Source looking for itself in the dark.

You are the fractal divine code.

You have always been the fractal divine code.

There is nothing outside of Source.

*

www.ingramcontent.com/pod-product-compliance
Lightning Source LLC
LaVergne TN
LVHW091035080826
845145LV00002B/508